THE REALIST FILM UNIT
IN COLD WAR AUSTRALIA
JOHN HUGHES

Published by John Hughes, Early Works and the Australian Teachers of Media Inc. (ATOM)

Copyright © 2013 John Hughes, Early Works

Every reasonable endeavour has been made to contact copyright holders. Where this has not been possible, the copyright holders are invited to contact the publisher.

All rights reserved. No part of this publication may be reproduced, stored in a retrieval system or transmitted in any form or by any means, electronic, mechanical, photocopying, recording or otherwise, without the prior written permission of the copyright owner.

ISBN 978-1-74295-328-1

Project Manager: Penelope Chai
Design: William Head, Yay Tractor
www.yaytractor.com

This project was supported by the City of Melbourne Writing About Melbourne Arts Grants Program.

Promoting 21st Century Democratic, Ecological Socialism

This project was supported by the Search Foundation

AUSTRALIAN TEACHERS OF MEDIA

CONTENTS

Acknowledgments iv
Preface vii
Introduction: Deane Williams ix

THE ARCHIVE PROJECT SCREENPLAY

Chapter 1 Days of hope 3
Chapter 2 Workers' art 19
Chapter 3 The early films: "realism" 29
Chapter 4 These are our children 37
Chapter 5 Screenings 43
Chapter 6 "Adversely known" 49
Chapter 7 Prices and the people 57
Chapter 8 A politics of fear 69
Chapter 9 Phone taps and number plates . . . 81
Chapter 10 Vote 'No'! 91
Chapter 11 They chose peace 101
Chapter 12 After '56 115

INTERVIEWS

Phillip Adams 123
Dick Mason 124
Don Munro 126
Dot Thompson 127
Margaret Walker 128

Realist Film Association Screenings 1945-59 . . 129

ACKNOWLEDGEMENTS

Thanks are due to the National Film and Sound Archive and the Australian Film Commission (now Screen Australia) for invaluable support in kind and in cash during the development of the feature documentary *The Archive Project*. The Australian Centre for the Moving Image (ACMI) and the post-production studio Music and Effects (M & E) in Melbourne also offered invaluable contributions. ACMI provided an artist in residence desk during the first phase of the project; this resulted in an installation at ACMI during their 2006 Contemporary Commonwealth exhibition. Music and Effects contributed a huge amount of work over an extended period at generously reduced rates. For this support I would like to thank in particular Emma Bortignon, Cynthia Mann, Doron Kipen and Keith Thomas at M&E. ABC TV Arts provided the film a modest television pre-sale at a crucial moment in the project, without which the film could not have been made, and for which I would like to thank Amanda Duthie and Courtney Gibson. This television pre-sale enabled Film Victoria to consolidate their development support with a production investment, and for this I would like to thank Steve Warne. The Australian Film Commission was supportive throughout; I take this opportunity to thank Karin Altmann, Lori Flekser, Jackie McKimmie and Stephen Wallace, and at the National Film and Sound Archive Ken Berryman, Helen Tully and Zsuzsi Szucs.

A huge number of people have generously donated their time and skills in the course of the project's development and production. Many of them are acknowledged in the credits of the film and the DVD. In particular though let me thank Sophia Gollan and Jodie Harris who helped work out what the New Theatre actors were probably saying in the Realist films that were made originally without sync dialogue. Also heartfelt thanks go to Bryan Brown, Nicos Lathouris, Mark Rogers and Louise Smith, who did the post-sync voices at Andrew Plain's Huzzah Sound recording studio in Sydney, the sound studio and everyone's time was generously donated to the project.

The primary creative collaborators have been film editor and co-director Uri Mizrahi, producer Philippa Campey, and Tim Patterson, whose design, graphics, and authoring skills on the DVD box set over many weekends are very much appreciated. This DVD box set includes the feature documentary *The Archive Project* 2006 (disc 1), films made by the Realist Film Unit, with alternative sound tracks where we have remade these (disc 2) and a series of illustrated oral history interviews (disc 3).

Uri Mizrahi's screen design collage provide much more than illustration to the screenplay.

My deepest debt is to those whose dedication created the films and sustained the Realist movement in Melbourne and later the Waterside Workers' Federation Film Unit in Sydney. In the exhausting task of compiling the Melbourne Realists exhibition schedule (1946-58), my thanks go to Lucy Demant, Matt Stephensen and especially Lucy Wright. I am also indebted to Elizabeth Coldicutt, Gerry Harant, Sue Mathews and to Rilke Muir and David Muir for their support over many years and permissions to reproduce material from their archives. Thanks to Ed Schefferle and Jan Blake for permission to reproduce stills from their collections. Staffs of the Australian National University's Noel Butlin Archive, the National Archives of Australia, the National Library of Australia and Melbourne University Archives have all been consistently helpful, patient and courteous.

In making the book I am grateful for the support of Avril McQueen and the City of Melbourne who encouraged the project with a grant from their 'Writing about Melbourne' program in 2011. For timely subsidy to printing costs I thank Peter Murphy and the Search Foundation. And for their generous creativity Penelope Chai and William Head; Penny for her organisational help and William for his design work.

John Hughes, Melbourne, July 2013

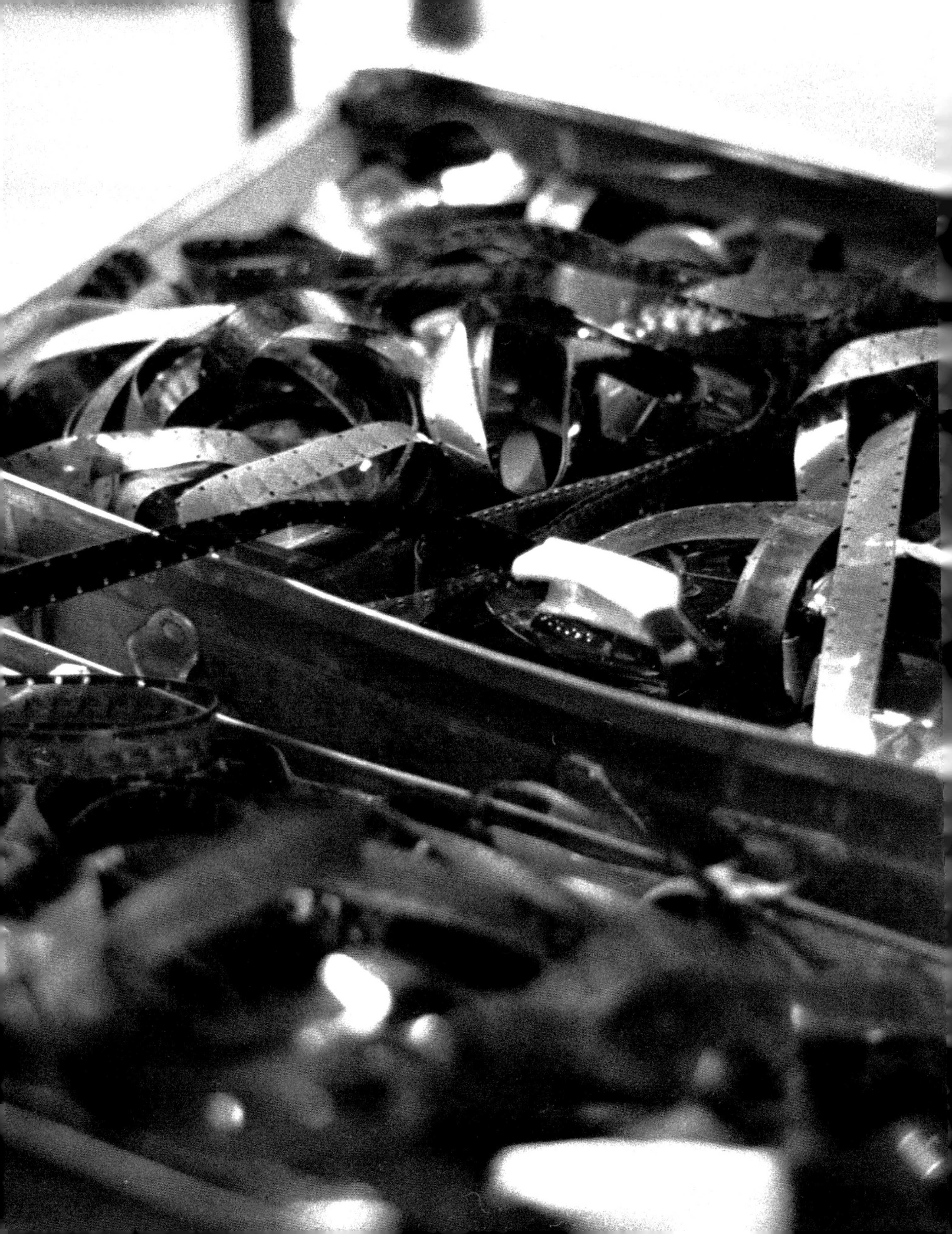

PREFACE

Over recent years audiences of film and television have sought to locate the 'real' in varieties of internet based media, television 'reality' formats and the moving image; 'documentary' is the tradition that most immediately responds. There has been a significant surge in audiences for documentary in both television and cinemas here in Australia and elsewhere. Over recent years a specialised scholarship has developed with new undergraduate courses, post-graduate studies and specialist periodicals and books for tertiary students in many languages.

Popular documentary across a spectrum from the polemical advocacy through to the more reflective and insightful sociological, observational works of Australia's Tom Zubrycki or dynamic investigative work like *Forbidden Lie$* (Anna Broinowski, Australia, 2007), *The President versus David Hicks* (Curtis Levy and Bentley Dean, Australia, 2006) deliver audiences a sense of connection with ideas and viewpoints that challenge the conservative orthodoxy of mainstream media. However 'mainstream media' has also articulated a kind of jargon of authenticity arguably meeting a closely related appetite.

For some, 'reality television' has delivered a response to this appetite for the 'authentic' transparent moment, combined with the fascination with celebrity; for others a critical, polemical documentary cinema has re-emerged to engage audiences with debates around contemporary political and social problems. The Realist film movement of the 1940s and 1950s is recognisable today as a kind of prophecy of many of the imperatives and dilemmas experienced by an engaged film culture at the beginning of the 21st century.

The 'fall of the wall' and corresponding re-alignments of global power, new challenges for democratic political culture and increased access to archives around the world all contribute to revision and reassessment of the culture wars that were constituted by the incommensurate world views that animated cultural and political behaviour during the second half of the 20th century. The story of the Melbourne Realists provides insight into these global questions as they were played out in the microcosm of a very local Australian story.

John Hughes, Melbourne, July 2013

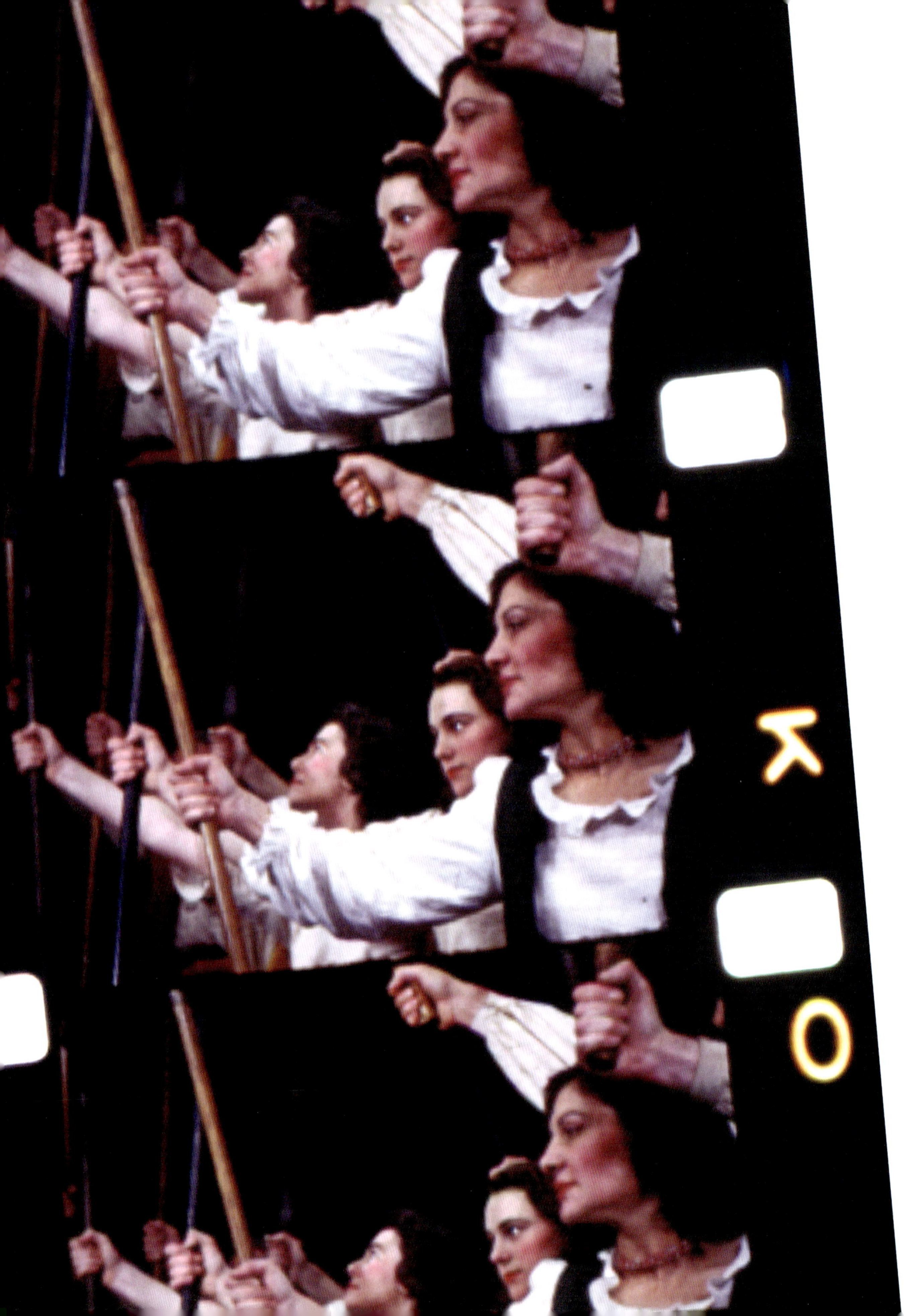
K
O

INTRODUCTION

> In the fields with which we are concerned, knowledge comes only in lightning flashes. The text is the long roll of thunder that follows.
> Walter Benjamin *The Arcades Project*[1]

Towards the end of *The Archive Project*, we accompany the film to Melbourne's Australian Centre for the Moving Image (ACMI) to see a number of events that accompanied the screening of some of the Realist Film Unit and other political films. We hear John Flaus voice the live narration for *These Are Our Children* (1947), and Elizabeth Coldicutt speaking about Ken Coldicutt's vision for film realism.[2] This audio-vision, Elizabeth Coldicutt recalling her experiences with the Realists at a lectern at ACMI, the institutionalised, governmental site for film and media culture draws these traditions together at the home of Australia's most prominent of film societies, Melbourne Cinémathèque, of the Melbourne International Film Festival, the *The Archive Project* and back to the State Film Centre and Realist Film Association. Elizabeth Coldicutt's image is allusive and intriguing, a dialectical image in this context, particularly in relation to another image of her that adorns the cover to this book. This image is at the heart of *The Archive Project* illuminating its purpose and its strategy.

Elizabeth Coldicutt (née Betty Lacey) was a member – of the Realist Film Unit/Association – alongside Ken Coldicutt, Gerry Harant and Bob Mathews at the same time as she worked at Victoria's State Film Centre alongside Chief Executive Neil Edwards, helping to import that Library's invaluable 16mm film collection now part of Australia's National Film and Sound Archive and the Centre's Film Literature Library. She was a founder of the Melbourne University Film Society and worked alongside Ken Coldicutt and Gerry Harant on the Olinda Film Festival and wrote on the Centre's activities for Film Monthly and Film Guide.[3]

The Realist Film Unit emerged from the 1930s international cultural responses to Fascism. These included the network of workers' theatre, literary and film organisations such as the German Workers International Relief, the New York Workers' Film and Photo League, the Spanish Relief Committee (SRC) and Friends of the Soviet Union (FSU). Australian mirror organisations included Workers' Art Clubs in Melbourne and Sydney, Melbourne's Workers' Theatre Group and after the war the Realist Film Unit.

Already self-educated in film theory and criticism, Ken Coldicutt began his political film activism in 1935 by helping Friends of the Soviet Union with the importation and screenings of Soviet films. It is likely that he

---

[1] Walter Benjamin. *The Arcades Project*. Trans. Howard Eiland and Kevin McLaughlin. Cambridge, Mass. and London. The Belknap Press of Harvard University Press, 2002: 456.

[2] This event was *The Independent Voice: Australian Political Documentary From the 1940s to the 1980s* screening July 13, 2005 curated by John Hughes and presented by the National Film and Sound Archive and Melbourne Cinémathèque at ACMI. Films featured were the Realist Film Unit's *These are Our Children* (1947), *Prices and the People* (1946), Margot Nash and Robin Laurie's *We Aim to Please (As If)* (1977) and Rod Bishop, Scott Murray and Gordon Glenn's *Beginnings* (1971).

[3] "From Radar Screen to Film Library" in *The Age*. 14 June 1950.

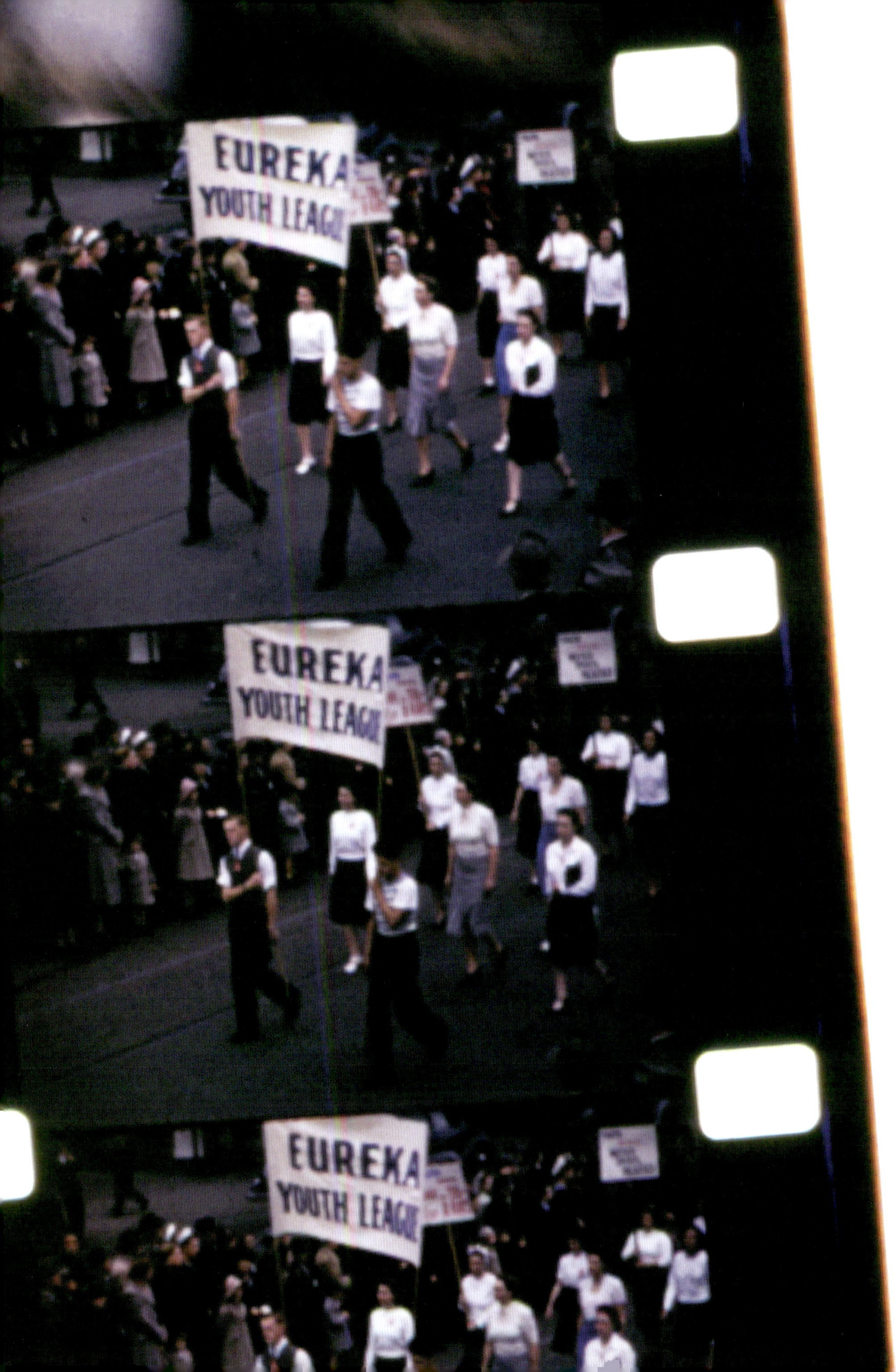
EUREKA
YOUTH LEAGUE

imported into Australia what are said to be the first prints of Eisenstein's *Ten Days That Shook The World* in 1936.[4]

In 1937 Coldicutt left FOSU to embark on the remarkable activist role as national film organiser for the Spanish Relief Committee. Amira Inglis tells us that he convinced the Committee to buy one of the first 16mm sound projectors imported into Australia, and he toured the Melbourne suburbs and country towns of Victoria with that machine. In early 1937/9, Coldicutt tells us, he set off on a tour of the east coast of Australia where 25,000 people in Victoria, New South Wales and Queensland saw the films and Coldicutt travelled 8,851 kilometres raising £500 for the SRC. These screenings are remarkable given the cumbersome equipment of the time and that the journeys were taken by rail.[5]

Ken Coldicutt maintained a strong cinematic aspect to this cultural network by reading and corresponding with film journals of the 1930s such as *Experimental Cinema*, *Close Up*, *Film*, *Film Art*, *Cinema*, *Cinema Quarterly*, *Sight and Sound*, and *New Theatre and Film*. These journals not only provided access to the burgeoning world of film criticism they also aided Coldicutt in his later programming of the Realist screenings and events because he could obtain reviews, details of film titles, names of distributors and writings on films from around the world. Coldicutt also wrote some of the earliest Australian commentary on the Soviet Cinema in his articles on 'Turksib: Building a Railroad and 'Cinema and Capitalism.[6]

Like Coldicutt, Bob Mathews became involved in political activism through the Unemployed Workers' Club and the Workers' Theatre Club in Brunswick in Melbourne's inner north. These clubs made available publications like *Proletariat*, *Stream* and *War What For?* immediately involving Mathews in the international network of workers' literature and theatre. In the late 1930s the Workers' Theatre Club evolved into New Theatre, including its association with its London cousin, and began importing plays such as Clifford Odets' *Till the Day I Die* and *Waiting for Lefty*. Mathews quite clearly understood his work with the Theatre as political action. He tells us in *The Archive Project* that towards 1945 he "wasn't satisfied with theatre production, and wanted to get closer to reality". Film seemed a logical medium for this so he bought a 16mm camera. As his interest shifted into film production, his friendship with Ted Cranstone, a photographer with the Works Department and later a highly regarded Department of Information camera operator working on John Heyer's *Born in the Sun* (1947) and *Men and Mobs* (1947), led to the initial screenings at New Theatre at 92 Flinders Street, Melbourne.

---

[4] "Sergei Eisenstein" *The Guardian*. (March 1948): 12

[5] Amira Inglis. *Australians in the Spanish Civil War*, Sydney: Allen and Unwin, 1987, 91.

[6] Ken Coldicutt. "Cinema and Capitalism." *Proletariat*: University Labor Club Magazine. (April/June 1935): 11-15.
— "Turksib: Building a Railroad." *The Documentary Tradition*. Ed. Lewis Jacobs. 2nd. ed. New York and London. W.W. Norton. 1979. 45-48.
For a contextualising of Coldicutt's writing see Deane Williams *Australian Post-War Documentary Films: An Arc of Mirrors*. Bristol and Chicago, Intellect, 2008.

Gerry Harant was an important member of the both New Theatre and the Realist Film Unit, his technical expertise in maintaining and preparing everything from stage equipment, such as lights and sound projection, to cameras and projectors allowed the Realist Film Unit/Association to continue its activities.

Coldicutt, Mathews, Coldicutt and Harant set about a program of filmmaking supported by the screenings on weekends so as to avoid interfering with the New Theatre stage productions. Three film works produced by the Realist Film Unit – *A Place to Live* (1946), *In My Beginning* (1947) and *Prices and the People* (1948) – as well as two films made for the Brotherhood of St. Laurence – *Beautiful Melbourne* (1947) and *These are Our Children* (1947) – display the common formal and ideological concerns of the international left employing a simple 'dialectical' principle, following Sergei Eisenstein, of putting two ideas in conflict with each other.

Utilising Ken Coldicutt's knowledge of the broader world of film distribution, including the films available through embassies and other cultural organisations, the Realists screened a large variety of films from all over the globe. These included *Battleship Potemkin* (Sergei Eisenstein, USSR, 1925), *Earth* (Alexander Dovzhenko, USSR, 1930), *Metropolis* (Fritz Lang, Germany, 1937), Michael Powell's *The Edge of the World* (UK, 1937) and Chaplin shorts, as well as documentaries like *Grass: A Nation's Battle for Life* (Merian C. Cooper and Ernest Schoedsack, USA, 1925), *Indonesia Calling* (Joris Ivens, 1945), *The City* (Ralph Steiner and Willard Van Dyke, USA, 1939), *There's No Future In it* (Leslie Fenton, UK, 1943) and Cecil Holmes' *Fighting Back* (New Zealand, 1948).

The Realists insisted that their production and screening activities be supported by the education of audiences in the critical appreciation of the film medium. These discussions occurred at New Theatre as well as members' houses.[7] One general title for a prominent series was 'The dialectics of cinema'. Others included 'Eisenstein's thesis that the principle of montage can be found in the creative process in all the arts' to 'The technique of the Maya Deren films'. Other topics included 'The films of Roberto Rossellini', 'Post-war French films seen in Melbourne' and 'The origins and development of cinema from the technical, economic, and social points of view'. These discussion groups provided audiences with the critical and historical background necessary for building a knowledgeable and engaged film culture, albeit one informed by a political activism.

While the Realists have existed under the title of Communist film unit, or political film activists, this titling has diminished their interconnectedness, influence and the nature of their political force. While the Realists were members of the Communist Party this attribution shouldn't be allowed to diminish their contribution to Australian film culture. While Ken Coldicutt's enormous efforts for the Spanish Relief Committee and the Realists conducting of screenings and discussion groups are potent examples, Elizabeth Coldicutt's affinities with the university, the Realists and the State Film Centre invokes the whole constellation of film culture in Melbourne: official, independent, radical, left, right, metropolitan, rural and suburban, historical and discursive.

---

[7] *Realist Film News*, October 1950.

To return to ACMI: Elizabeth Coldicutt's audio-image is also emblematic of John Hughes' method of montage in *The Archive Project*; an historically contingent accounting for the meanings inherent not only in this specific historical moment but also the possibilities available in adopting the montage method favoured by Ken Coldicutt's mentor Eisenstein. As Anne Nesbet tells us, Eisenstein, like Walter Benjamin, "could appreciate the power of 'profane illumination', the revelation of a juncture between seemingly disparate objects or epochs".[8] For Nesbet, this 'montage-based approach to philosophy', encapsulated by Eisenstein's 'Montage of Attractions' and Benjamin's *The Arcades Project (Passagenwerk)*, hinges on the similarity between Eisenstein's reflex art, a "real chain of cause and effect that would nullify the distance between the screen and the brain" and Benjamin's montage of shocks, of images, quotes and aphorisms that would characterise his *Passagenwerk*.[9] Both Eisenstein and Benjamin sought to enable the incorporation of the image into philosophy, to direct an imagistic way of thinking. Drawing on both these traditions *The Archive Project*, in its own audio-vision, emulates the kind of (dialectical) thinking proposed by Eisenstein and Benjamin, a thoughtful materialism that brings together the past and its future.

Deane Williams, Melbourne 2012
Associate Professor, School of English, Communications and Performance Studies, Monash University

---

8 Anne Nesbet. *Savage Junctures: Sergei Eisenstein and the Shape of Thinking*, London and New York, 2007: 9-10.
9 Nesbet. *Savage Junctures*: 8-9.

THE ARCHIVE PROJECT
96 MINUTES, AUSTRALIA, 2006

CHAPTER 1

DAYS OF HOPE

KEITH GOW (1921-1987)

Keith's career began as a theatre director, designer and actor for the Newcastle Workers' Theatre and later the New Theatre in Sydney. One of his earliest film projects was as a cinematographer with Bob Mathews, David Muir and others on the Realists' *They Chose Peace* (1952). Keith Gow, Jock Levy and Norma Disher established a theatre on the Sydney docks called The Maritime Industries Theatre (MIT). They made a 16mm trailer to advertise the MIT's first production Ewan MacColl's *The Travelers* (1953). The success of the trailer led to the formation of the Waterside Workers Federation Film Unit (1953-8). The WWF Film Unit produced 11 films for a number of trade unions including the classic documentaries *The Hungry Miles* (1954) and *Hewers of Coal* (1957).

In 1959 Keith joined the Commonwealth Film Unit (later to become Film Australia) working as senior cameraman, director and producer. He co-wrote *The Cars That Ate Paris* (1974) with Peter Weir and Piers Davies. He made about eighteen films at Film Australia; including as director *Australian Geography* (1970), *Our Asian Neighbors* (1975), *And Their Ghosts May Be Heard* (1975), *History of Australian Cinema 1930 - 1940* (1979), *TV Law Series* (1980), *Women of Utopia* (1983) and *The Human Face of Russia* (1984), and as cinematographer *The Builder* (1959), *From the Tropics to the Snow* (1962), *Change at Groote* (1968), *The Line* (1970) and *Big Island* (1970).

Picture: Keith Gow and Jock Levy with the wind up Bolex, on the set of *Film-Work, Glebe* (1979).

Fade up from black. A projected 16mm image is occupying a portion of the frame. We see the texture of film leader superimposed on the image of Keith Gow, holding a couple of film cans under his arm, walking toward camera as it tracks back. In voiceover we hear.

KEITH GOW   (V/0)

Any film is propaganda of one sort or another. It always contains a point of view, a message of some sort. It can't be otherwise.

The sound of a film editing machine button accompanies a freeze of the tracking shot. Screen design elements evoke a torn page.

NARRATOR

One place to start piecing together a story of the Melbourne Realist Film Unit is here, with filmmaker Keith Gow.

The snap of a clapperboard marking a sync point is removed from the frame, revealing three people at an editing bench. These are the members of the Waterside Workers Federation Film Unit (1953-58), Norma Disher, Keith Gow and Jock Levy. This, like the first scene is an excerpt from *Film-Work* (1981). We see the animated title: *Film-Work* resolve itself from fragments evoking single 16mm film frames.

NARRATOR

I interviewed Keith in the 1970s for Film-Work, a documentary I made on the Waterside Workers Federation Film Unit. They made some wonderful classic films with Australian trade unions during the 1950s.

From *Film-Work* we see Keith at an editing bench. In reverse angle we see the editing bench screen with the projected image of young, determined waterside workers: voting workers 'taking positive action'.

Keith Gow in Film-Work (1979) *in* The Archive Project (2006)

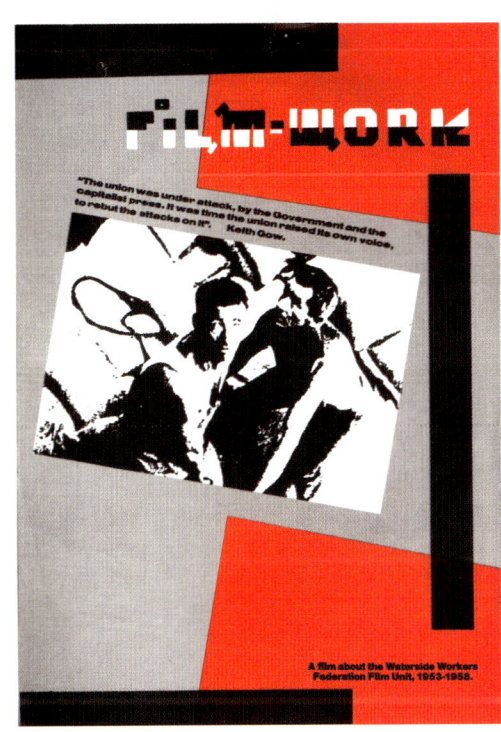

Film-Work *poster (Carol P.T., 1981)*

May Day, Melbourne (1946). Bob Mathews

Returning to the tracking shot from *Film-Work* with Keith in the corridor at Film Australia, we see overlay images as young hands thread a 16mm camera, a photograph of Keith filming with a Bolex at a demonstration in Sydney in the early 1950s.

KEITH GOW   (V/O)

The first time I was ever able to actually use the tools of filmmaking myself was in the early '50s when Bob Mathews of the Realist film organisation in Melbourne asked me to do some photography on a film about the Peace Movement.

Cut to a production still showing Margot Nash, cinematographer, and John Whitteron, sound recordist, aboard Keith Gow's motorcycle sidecar shooting *Film-Work*, at the entrance to Film Australia's Lindfield studios, Sydney, 1979.

NARRATOR

When Keith says –

KEITH GOW   (V/O)

…the Realist film organisation in Melbourne…

Screen design collage flips from the *Film-Work* production still to documents and stills illustrating an introduction to the Melbourne Realist film movement.

NARRATOR

He signals a story that Film-Work didn't tell. The story of the Realist film organisation is a story of a small group of dedicated people. They were pioneers in giving Australian audiences access to the images and ideas of world cinema, beyond British and American commercial distribution.

They started making films around 1945. Some are lost, others exist only in fragments.

Jock Levy directs a rehearsal of A Sky Without Birds, *New Theatre Sydney, 1952 (from* They Chose Peace, *1952)*

In Sydney Jock Levy had 'creative differences' with the New Theatre around Oriel Gray's play, A Sky without Birds, *the play he directed for the New Theatre to coincide with the Carnival for Peace and Friendship, 1952.*

JOCK LEVY (OA)

Jock is one of the generation who became committed to the left through his involvement with community theatre in the 1930s. In his case the formative experience was the Jewish Youth Theatre in Sydney. As a worker on the Sydney wharf since the 1940s, Jock initiated the Maritime Industries Theatre in 1953 with Keith Gow and Norma Disher and the Sydney branch of the Waterside Workers Federation (now MUA) and following this, the Waterside Workers Federation Film Unit. As an actor Jock Levy's performance in the WWF Film Unit's comedy *Four's a Crowd*, 1955, and later with the Commonwealth Film Unit productions (e.g. *Where Dead Men Lie*, 1971) and the films of Australian maverick producers and directors such as Cecil Holmes (e.g. *Three in One*, 1956) is highly regarded. From the mid 1960s he earned his living driving taxis. In 2010 Jock was awarded an Order of Australia for his contribution to the Australian film industry.

See *Film-Work*, John Hughes, 1981 on the Waterside Workers Federation Film Unit. Lisa Milner, *Fighting Films: a history of the Waterside Workers' Federation Film Unit*, Pluto Press (2003).

NORMA DISHER

Norma came down to Sydney from Bega before World War 2 and took up a job in the music library at Radio 2GB. It wasn't long before she became involved with the New Theatre, a creative endeavour she remained committed to for half a century. It was there she met Jock Levy and Keith Gow; together they established the Maritime Industries Theatre on the Sydney waterfront, in collaboration with the arts program of the Waterside Workers Federation. In 1954 they staged Ewen McCall's *The Travellers*. A 16mm film trailer made to advertise the play led to their first documentary WWF Film Unit's *Pensions for Veterans*, a film supporting the union's industrial campaign. Norma worked fulltime for the Miscellaneous Workers Union (MWU) and nights and weekends unpaid with the New Theatre, and with Jock and Keith on the WWF Film Unit. She came onto the payroll with the Film Unit for their Building Workers Industrial Union (BWIU) film *Bones of Building* (1956). Norma worked with distributor Eddie Allison at Quality Films, and supported the work on the Sydney Realist Film Association. After the Film Unit folded in 1958, Norma returned to the 'Missos' (MWU), first in the NSW office and later with the Federal Branch as a Secretary to Ray Gietzelt. Norma continued her work with the New Theatre, committee work, directing and a variety of community-based organisations.

See 'Interview with Norma Disher', Margot Nash and Margot Oliver, *Lip* 1980: 134-138.

WATERSIDE WORKERS FEDERATION FILM UNIT

The Waterside Workers Federation Film Unit (1953-8) was established on the Sydney docks following on from the Maritime Industries Theatre (1953) and the trailer that the Unit's members made to advertise their play *The Travellers* (Ewen McColl). The Unit's members Norma Disher, Keith Gow and Jock Levy all worked with the New Theatre in Sydney. Between 1953 and 1958 they made 11 films for a variety of trade unions, among them Australian documentary classics *The Hungry Miles* (1955), *November Victory* (1955) and *Hewers of Coal* (1957). The WWF Film Unit's success must partly be attributed to the fact that they were protected by a powerful trade union, while others (Cecil Holmes, Ken Coldicutt) were blacklisted. The WWF had experienced the potential of documentary film in advancing their policies when the Dutch filmmaker Joris Ivens made *Indonesia Calling* with support from the maritime trade unions in 1945-6.

Keith Gow, sound recordist John Whitteron, cinematographer Margot Nash shooting Film-Work (1979) outside Film Australia, Eton Road, Lindfield.

"...W.W.F. FILM UNIT... a recent issue of *Maritime Worker* (reports) the Federal Council of the Waterside Workers' Federation has endorsed the work its [NSW Branch] film unit and has authorised the purchase of additional equipment... The recent Warsaw Youth Festival ... awarded a gold medal to THE HUNGRY MILES. The unit, which is now working on a film for the Building Workers' Industrial Union, intends to increase its mobile activities." Extract from *Realist Film News*, November-December, 1955.

Pensions for Veterans, WWF, 1953. *The Hungry Miles*, WWF, 1955. *November Victory*, WWF, 1955. *Bones of Building*, BWIU, 1956. *WWF Newsreel*, WWF, 1956. *Banners Held High*, NSW May Day Committee, 1956. *Hewers of Coal*, Miners Federation, 1957. *Four's a Crowd*, WWF, 1957. *The Housing Problem and You*, BWIU, 1957. *Think Twice*, Boilermakers Union, 1957. *Not Only the Need*, BWIU, 1958 (updated version of *The Housing Problem and You*)

A box set of WWF Film Unit films is available from the Maritime Union of Austsralia (MUA). See also: *Film-Work*, John Hughes, 1981: Lisa Milner, *Fighting Films: A history of the Waterside Workers Federation Film Unit*, 2003, Pluto Press: Waterside Workers Federation Collection E211/163, Noel Butlin Archives, ANU, Canberra.

ASIO (Australian Security Intelligence Organisation) surveillance photographs show Keith Gow shooting a scene for the Realist film *They Chose Peace*. The photograph shows a small crowd greeting passengers from a ship on a Sydney wharf.

NARRATOR

Their contribution to film culture didn't meet with favour from governments of their time.

One of the Melbourne Realists, Bob Mathews, handed the camera to Keith Gow in 1952.

A slow zoom in to the ASIO photograph features Bob Mathews, dominant in the shot, holding a reflector board, watching as delegates to the 1952 Sydney Youth Carnival for Peace and Friendship prepare to approach the gangplank.

Cut to a sequence from *Film-Work*: Keith is being interviewed in his Film Australia office. He holds a spring wind Bolex. As the dialogue proceeds Keith 'buttons-on'.

KEITH GOW   (V/O)

The advice that was given to me by Bob Mathews was 'get it running, quickly' because things happen fast and by the time you fiddle around with it, it might be all over. So in fact that was very good advice and that's what I've always remembered. You know you switch it on – you're shooting.

Sequence from *Film-Work* continues as we cut to the p.o.v. of Keith's Bolex, swinging to the film crew shooting the interview. The image freezes on the filmmaker narrator John Hughes.

NARRATOR

Another place to start is with the trims I've been carrying around for years. These two battered attaché cases have taken over 20 years to unpack.

Screen design collage with black and white stills of the "two battered attaché cases", both open and closed, showing the condition of the film that was handed-on in the early 1980s.

Film-Work, *cinematographer Margot Nash. Cut to Keith Gow in his Film Australia office.*

Picture: Keith Gow (behind Bolex) and Bob Mathews (gesturing), ASIO surveillance photograph, 1952.

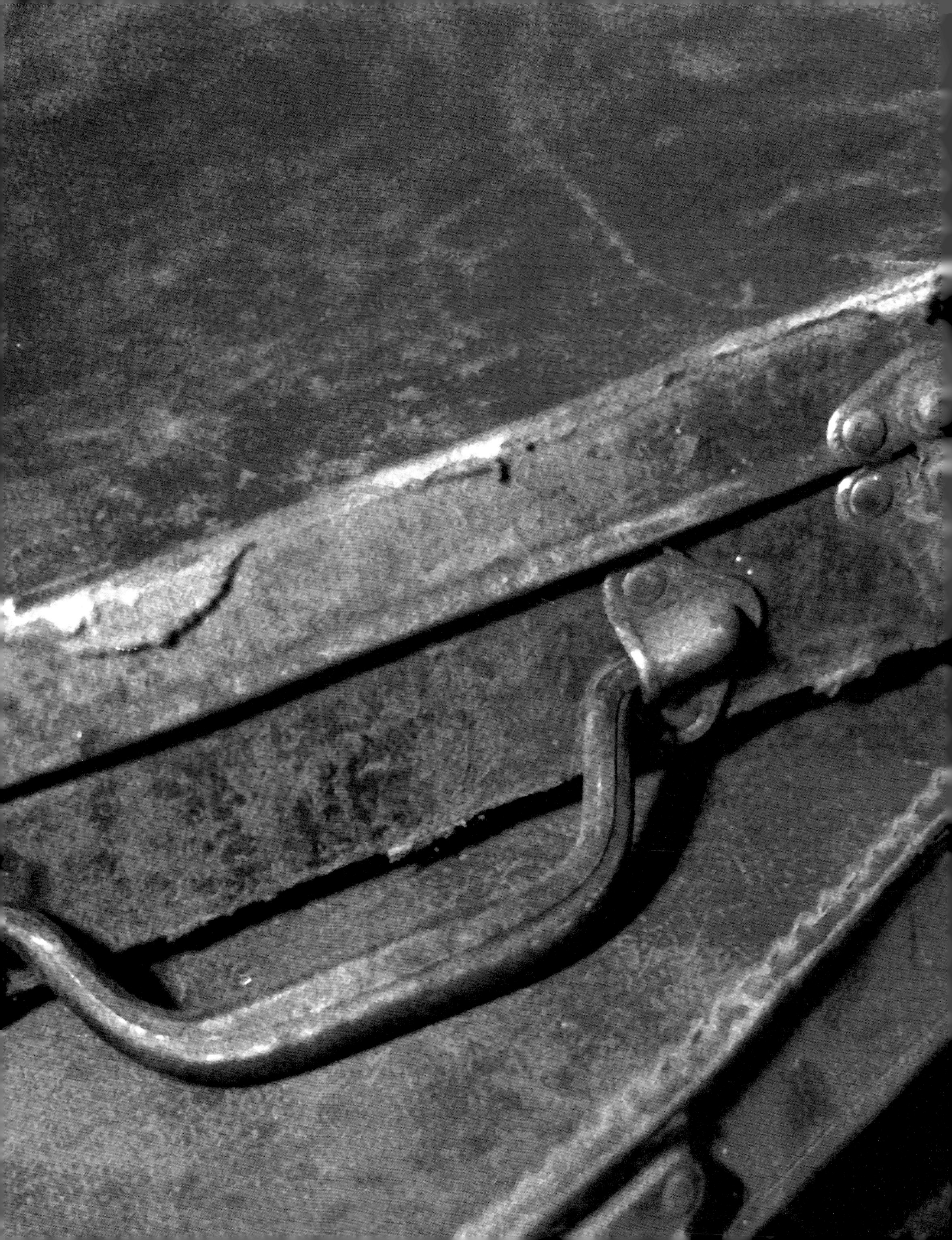

They were handed to me in the early 1980s as I searched for the missing archives of the Realist film movement. These trims and out-takes and files and documents have traveled with me from house to house, and film to film.

TITLE: THE ARCHIVE PROJECT

It's about time they came out of the closet.

SUPER:

'The wise and wicked art of re-editing the work of others'
Sergei Eisenstein, 1929

A montage of fragmentary, incoherent images (derived in fact from these "battered attaché cases").

NARRATOR

Out of the blue, the archives of Bob Mathews, one of the original founders of the Realist Film Unit had surfaced.

Stills of Bob Mathews daughter, Sue, unlocking the cellar under her Northcote house.

Bob's daughter Sue knew I was working on the Realist story. She called me to say that she had found Bob's home movies in the cellar.

SUE MATHEWS (V/O)

He didn't throw away anything, so we've got the - you know - splicing block and all sorts of things that probably have been no use to anyone for fifty years. But we've still got them.

From Bob Mathews home movie footage we see the young Rivka Mathews, Bob Mathews and Sue as a baby in a garden setting - classic home movie, new baby.

All of this stuff was in a room under Bob and Rivka's house at Donvale and when we packed up our parents' home a couple of months ago we brought it all over to the cellar under my house.

Colour and black and white home movie footage of the 1950s shows Bob and Rivka playing up for the camera, shadows of Rivka's dancing figure against the trunk of a tree, Bob throwing a picnic rug over the camera's lens, Bob nursing a baby (Susan), feeding her from a bottle.

SUE MATHEWS (V/O)

He is living in a nursing home, he has dementia, which is fairly advanced and unfortunately he can no longer tell us about any of this material.

Cut back to Sue Mathews speaking to camera.

He doesn't have any - if he has memories of it, he's not able to explain to us.

Sue carries boxes from the cellar. We see the boxes in the back of Sue's car. We see stills of Bob as a young man, and an older one.

NARRATOR

Bob's memory was gone but maybe some of the missing films might be among these cans.

From Bob's home movie footage we see the shadows of Rivka and Bob, Rivka waves.

Cut to Rita Parkinson, Film Archivist at the National Film and Sound Archive (Canberra) inspecting 16mm film.

NARRATOR

It's quite faded. It's got a really strong vinegar smell. So even though it's smelly and wrinkly and a bit faded in parts, it's still got some really beautiful images on it.

And they made good cement back then 'cause the splices are holding together pretty well. We're going to have to treat it kindly, be very gentle with it, look at all the bits of information that's in there, because all these little clues help us to discern what - what's on the film. Sometimes we can be left in the dark.

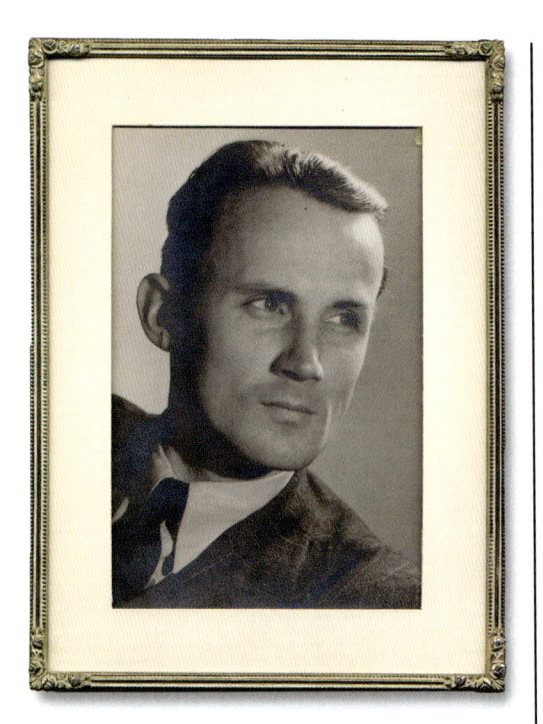

Bob Mathews, 1938.

Rita Parkinson examines Bob Mathews' footage at the National Film and Sound Archive in Canberra: "Aussies with flags".

Rita Parkinson carefully unwraps paper from a tightly rolled trim. She reads the label.

"Aussies with flags"

Highly saturated Kodachrome colour footage shows Melbourne University Labor Club and New Theatre marchers with banners, Melbourne, May Day, 1946. Collage with Bob Mathews publicity portrait, New Theatre.

NARRATOR

There is only one interview with Bob Mathews, recorded in the early 1990s on my high-8 video camera by film historian Deane Williams.

Bob Mathews interview, Deane Williams, 1993.

BOB MATHEWS

I was one of the production committee of the New Theatre and I was producing plays over - for quite a few years and had begun to think that this - you know this is not the way to go - we should be learning to make films.

Screen design incorporates countdown leader.

I wasn't satisfied with the theatre production, you know I wanted to get closer to reality.

From Bob Mathews home movies we see Bob dressed in a suit, lying on his back, holding his arms out with hands framing up a 'shot'.

NARRATOR

In these cans were reels of 16mm home movies, documentation of demonstrations and strikes in Melbourne in the 40s and 50s. Exquisite, evocative trims, off cuts and out-takes, tiny fragments of imagery, the previous generation's memories flashing back into the present moment.

"We should be learning to make films…"

"I wanted to get closer to reality,"
Bob Mathews

BOB MATHEWS 1911 – 2005

Robert (Bob) Mathews joined the New Theatre when it was the Workers Theatre in the early 1930s. Having left school at aged 14, Bob dated his commitment to left wing politics from seeing a family evicted from their home during the depression years. He was a foundation member, actor and director of some of the most successful of the early Workers' Theatre and New Theatre plays, including Clifford Odets *Waiting for Lefty* (1936), *Till the Day I Die* (1937), A. Afinogenev's *Distant Point* (1932) and J. B. Priestley's *They Came to a City* (1946).

The Realist film movement began with screenings at the New Theatre organised by Bob in late 1945. With Ken Coldicutt, Bob was one of the creative principals of the Realist Film Unit and Association, and with his partner Rivkah, was an activist in the peace movement. In 1956, along with many artists and intellectuals around the world, he turned away from the Communist Party at the time of the revelations of the 20th Congress of the Communist Party of the Soviet Union (February) and Russia's suppression of Hungary (October). Bob Mathews went on to be a successful businessman in the fashion industry, building the Witchery chain. He remained a supporter of the Melbourne Film Festival all his life. Records are held by the National Archives of Australia, the National Film and Sound Archives, and the Performing Arts Museum at the Victorian Arts Centre (New Theatre Collection).

In the National Film and Sound Archive's Melbourne office Sue Mathews winds through her fathers films on a Steenbeck editing bench.

NARRATOR

Among Sue's treasures were lost items from the Realist catalogue.

On the Steenbeck screen we see delegates on a tour in China, 1951.

SUE (O/S)

That's my mum there.

NARRATOR

There was Bob's film, A Glimpse of New China.

Shots from *A Glimpse of New China*, and *May Day 1946*, collage from New Theatre footage and the *Margaret Walker Dance Group 1946*.

NARRATOR

And there was also footage of May Day 1946. The filmmakers were part of a much broader movement of cultural activism; theatre, painting, literature, music and dance.

They responded to the desperation of the Depression and the rise of fascism in Europe. They wanted to help build a people's movement for peace and for a more humane society.

The Russian Revolution looked like a beacon to the future. Their cultural activism was inspired by their political dedication.

For them, 'realism' was an antidote to escapist fantasy. Making films was one part of their project. They also wanted Australian audiences to be able to see films that were otherwise not available, classic European and Russian cinema, avant-garde American film, British and Canadian documentary, Labor movement films, films with a purpose, art house movies.

BOB MATHEWS (V/O)

Well the absence of...

Bob Mathews interview.

> *...anything with real meaning was the thing, rather than what was coming out of Hollywood, although I resented Hollywood because of its cramping of the development of Australian cinema.*

Cut to: slow zoom in – the interior of a small cinema (Sydney Filmmakers Co-op, ex *Film-Work* outs), countdown leader projected on the screen.

> *The screening was the main reason for existence.*

Bob Mathews filming through the fence at a picket, circa 1947.

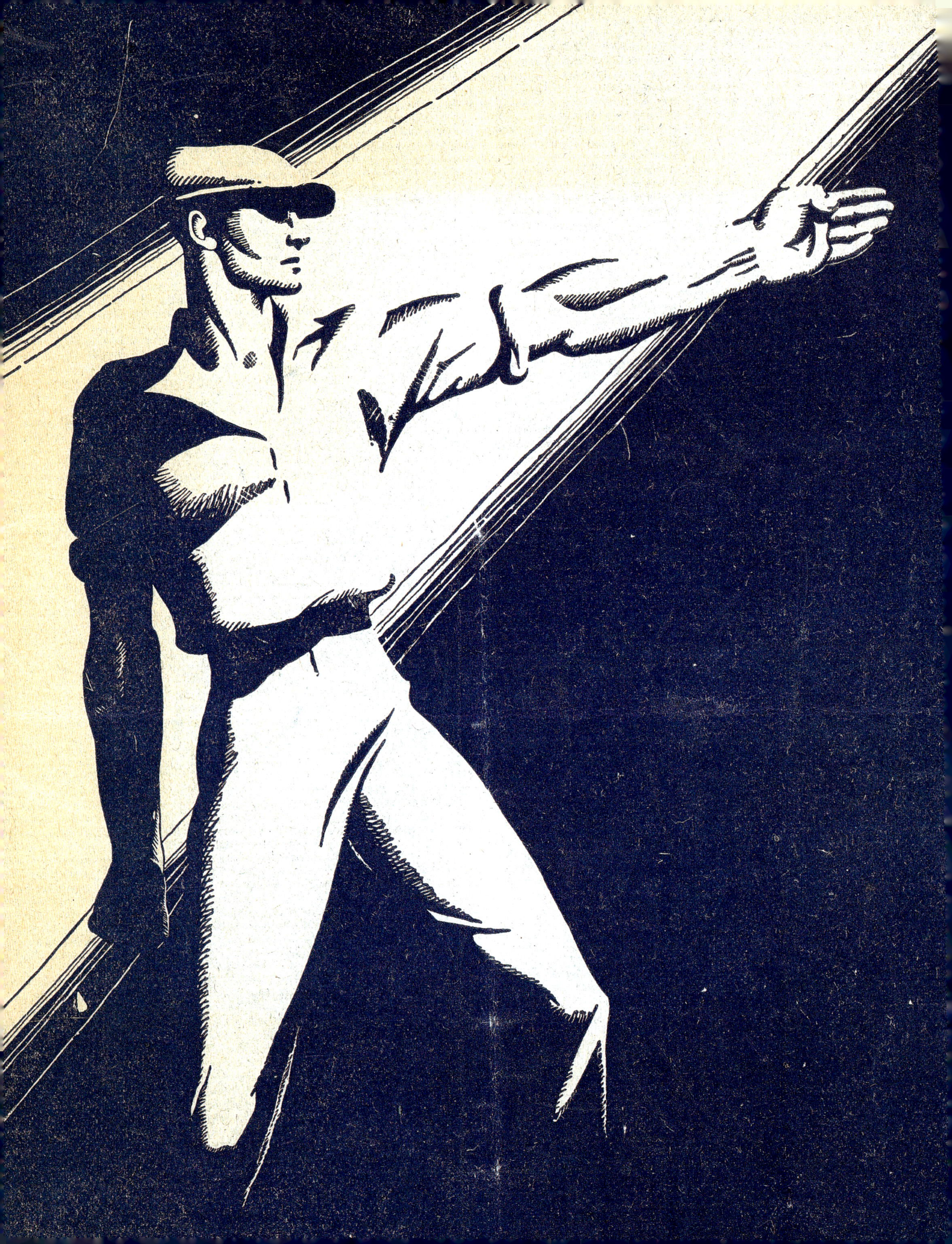

CHAPTER 2   WORKERS' ART

See: Amirah Inglis, Australians in the Spanish Civil War, *Allen & Unwin, 1987.* Deane Williams, 'Screening Coldicutt: introduction' *on-line journal* Screening the Past, *December 1997.*

Around the world Spanish Relief Committees were formed in 1936 to support the Spanish Republican Government's resistance to a military coup under General Franco, supported by Italian Fascist and German Nazi forces. Ken Coldicutt left his work as film organiser with the Movement Against War and Fascism and joined the Australian branch of the Spanish Relief Committee. He imported sound and silent films produced in Spain and London and organised and delivered screenings around the country, from Melbourne to Mossman, Queensland, from South Australia to as far south as Hobart. In May and June 1938, Ken organised screenings in 25 Queensland towns – in Innisfail alone 900 people attended. Queensland was the most successful location because of the numbers of Italian, Spanish and Yugoslav cane cutters who donated generously to the committee's work. In Melbourne's Assembly Hall 4000 people saw *They Shall Not Pass* (Spain, 1936) over seven nights in November 1937. During eight months of screenings, 25,000 people across Australian saw these films. This was the first time in Australia that films had been used as an organising tool in this way. Films screened included *News from Spain* (1937), *Attlee in Spain* (1937) *Modern Orphans of the Storm* (1937) *Behind Spanish Lines* (1938), *Help Spain*, *The Health of Spain*, *Defence of Madrid* (Ivor Montagu and the Progressive Film Unit, UK, 1936) and *They Shall Not Pass*.

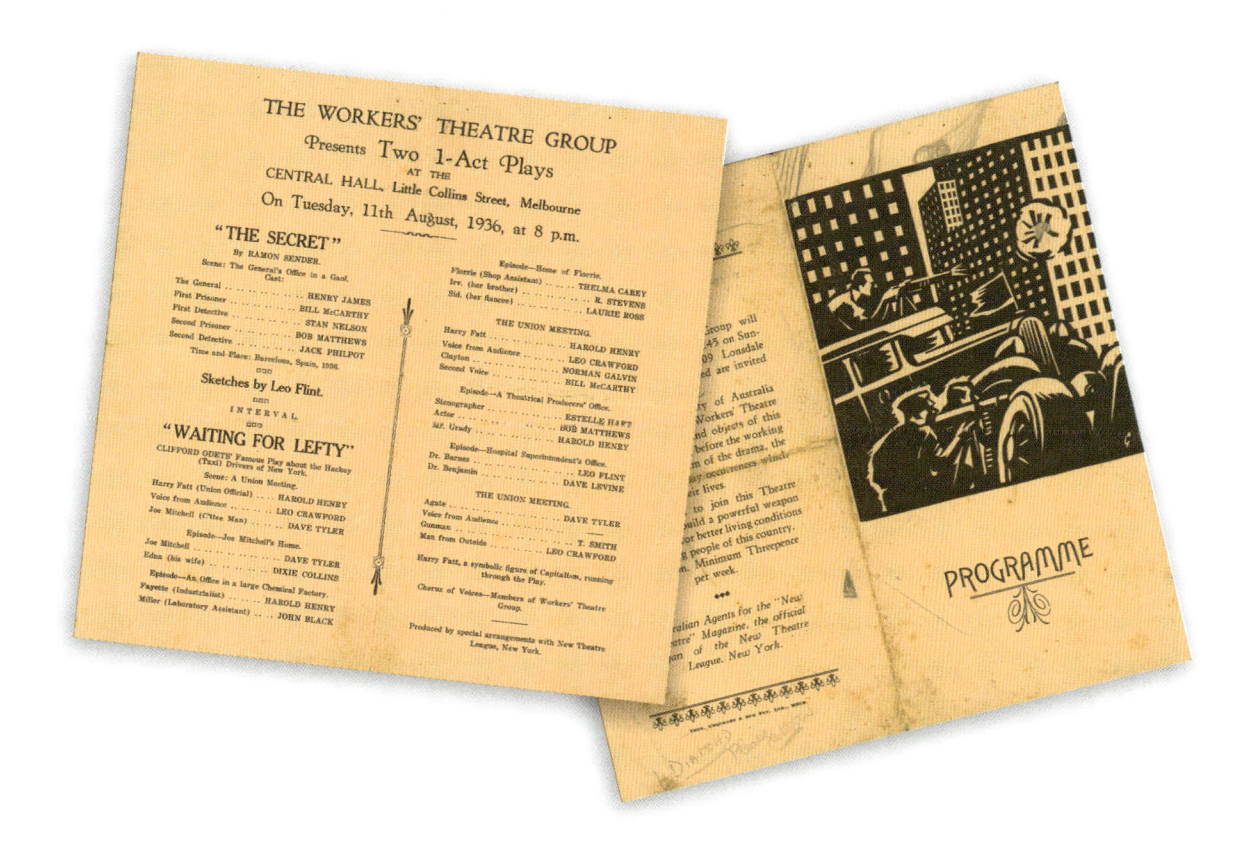

BOB MATHEWS

Then Ken Coldicutt turned up and discussed all the other possibilities that Ken knew about that we didn't.

Overlay montage: stills of Ken Coldicutt with images from his collection of posters and documents from when Ken was 'Films Officer' for the Victorian Branch of the Spanish Relief Committee.

Then we learned that Ken had carted a projector around all over Australia, I understand, on his own; you know what that means, with a transformer and a 16mm projector. He began doing this I think during the Spanish Civil War.

Ken Coldicutt's black and white home movie footage. Collage; Spanish Relief Committee files, the 'damaged' portrait from Ken's files, Proletariat.

Ken Coldicutt, editor Proletariat *(Labour Club, Melbourne University)*

NARRATOR

After his death in 1993 Ken's family had kept some 16mm home movies that he'd shot during the late 1940s and early 1950s and his files included documents and letters from the period of the Spanish Civil War. A lot of the old letters were very badly damaged. There remained traces of his correspondence with the International Spanish Relief Committee and British distributors of films on Spain.

As a student at Melbourne University in the early 30s, Ken Coldicutt edited the Labor Club's journal, Proletariat, *where he wrote about the power of the moving image. He joined the Communist Party on his 20th birthday.*

Film Poster *They Shall Not Pass* (1936) advertising a screening at Melbourne's Assembly Hall, November 19, 1937.

When the Spanish Civil War began, he joined the Spanish Relief Committee and traveled the length and breadth of the country. He showed films supporting the Republican Government that was desperately defending itself against a military coup of Spanish Fascists under Franco.

Stills; portraits Bob Mathews, Ken Coldicutt.

Bob Mathews joined the Workers Theatre through the Unemployed Workers' Union in Brunswick in the early 1930s. He acted, produced and directed anti-Fascist plays from the 1930s onwards. Ken spent the war years in the air force.

Superimposed scrolling graphic: Ken Coldicutt, interview, Wendy Lowenstein 1992, Oral History Collection, National Library of Australia.

KEN COLDICUTT (V/O)

I did what I'd always meant to do as soon as the war was over, that is to start this job of setting up a film organisation. And at New Theatre I contacted first Bob Mathews and later Gerry Harant.

I had three hundred pounds deferred pay and Bob Mathews decided to put in an equal amount; so we both put in three hundred pounds to establish the Realist Film Unit, which was in 1945.

Realist Film Unit document from Ken's papers: Registration of a Business Name: 'Realist Film Unit'.

The object of our screenings was not only to establish our name and fame, but also to accumulate funds for film making because the first objective of the Realist Film Unit was to produce films.

Newspaper cutting *The Guardian*, Melbourne, March 1946 'Realist Film Unit Show'. Using the attaché cases trims, scenes from Margaret Walker Dance Group and New Theatre 1946, a visual précis illustrates these early film projects of Bob Mathews and Ken Coldicutt. Their coverage evolves from documentation of staged action and more cinematic treatments of the action.

NARRATOR

The Realists documented a series of New Theatre productions in 1946. But their very first film is lost. They made a 20-minute color film about the Eureka Youth League Christmas Camp at the end of 1945 that they called **400 Film Stars**. *A delegation to a youth festival in Eastern Europe gave it away when they found they had no other gift to offer their hosts. The film must*

NEW THEATRE MELBOURNE, 1946

The New Theatre developed from the Melbourne Workers' Theatre of the 1930s. The New Theatre movement was Australia wide, and international. A history of the Melbourne New Theatre has been written by Angela O'Brien. The Melbourne New Theatre archives are held by the Performing Arts Museum, State Theatre, Melbourne. In late 1945 and 1946 the Realists filmed scenes from their performances.

See: Angela Hillel, New Theatre, *Melbourne 1936 – 1986, New Theatre, 1986.* Angela O'Brien, The Road Not Taken: Political and Performance Ideologies at Melbourne New Theatre, 1935-1960, *Ph. D, Monash, 1989.* Anon: The New Years: six decades of Sydney's radical New Theatre, *1992.*

NARRATOR (CONT.)

be there somewhere in the archives of the World Federation of Democratic Youth or buried in the Film Archives in Prague or Budapest.

The New Theatre was a community-based political theatre. It provided one of the few production outlets for Australian plays and it fostered new forms like the Australian Folk Musical. They did political satire, agitprop; they performed at factories and in street meetings.

Among their productions in 1946 was God Bless the Guv'nor, a burlesque send-up of 19th century melodrama.

White Justice, *Australian Aboriginal League with New Theatre*

NEW THEATRE PRODUCTIONS 1946

White Justice
A segment of Coming Our Way
Writers: New Theatre Collective
Written and performed with the collaboration of the Australian Aboriginal League, the dance theatre work is based on the research of The Guardian journalist Jim Crawford who broke the story of the 1946 stockman's strike in Western Australia's Pilbara region. This was the first strike by Aboriginal workers.
Dance performance: Eric Onus, Joyce McKinnon, Harold Bux, Edna Brown, Winifred Onus, Con Edwards, George McKinnon (from the Australian Aboriginal League) with Peter Sainthill, Colin Burns, Ian Fairley, Norma Russell, William Dye, William Anderson, Rex Lowe.

God Bless the Guv'nor
Ted Willis (Unity Theatre, London)
Ted Willis uses the 19th century burlesque form in a satirical take on the British class system.
Director: Hugh Esson | Producers: Bill Juliff and Bill Griffiths
Set Design: 'Vane' Lindsay | Lead actor: Bill Griffiths

Spanish Village
Lope de Vega (1562-1635)
17th century 'realism': Lope de Vega is credited with being the first dramatist to treat the 'common' people with dignity and strength.
Producer and Director: Hilda Esson
Dance choreography: Margaret Frey (Walker) | Set Design: Eva Harris
Costumes: Margaret Dietrich and Herta Schnierer | Sound: Gerry Harant

"With its ballet and music, its costumes, weapons and stage effects, (Spanish Village) was in many ways our most ambitious effort so far."
Hilda Esson, New Theatre Review, February-March, 1947

Tartuffe
Moliere (1622-73)
Moliere's Tartuffe was banned as seditious following its first performance in Louis XIV's Paris (1664). His comedies ridiculed the hypocrisy of the clergy and the pretensions of privilege.
Producer and Director: Hilda Esson | Set and Costume Design: 'Vane' Lindsay
Lead players: Yvonne Taylor, Bruce Beeby, Jack Phillips and Felix Farquharson

"It is precisely because Moliere's comedies reflect an acute observation of the society of his own time that his work has more reality for us today than that of his many illustrious contemporaries."
Aileen Palmer, New Theatre Review, July 1946

They Came to a City
JB Priestley (1894-1984)
In Priestley's play, nine characters find themselves outside the gates of a utopian city. Faced with the choice of entering this new world or remaining in the old one, two people decide to stay, in order to fight for a better world for all.
Producer and Director: Robert 'Bob' Mathews
Stage design: 'Vane' Lindsay | Lighting: Gerry Harant
Cast: Marjorie Forbes, Dora Norwood, William Phillips, Joyce Addison, Les Davey, Norma Ferris, Ken Otway, Shirey Robertson, Colin Burns

Love on the Dole
Writers: Ronald Gow and Walter Greenwood
Producers: Shirley Robinson and Dora Norwood | Set Design: 'Vane' Lindsay

Cast: Sheila Glass, Charlotte Hinton, Bill Griffiths, Alf Jones, Charles McCormack, Sally Darnley, Susan Saffir, Nancy Fryberg, Charles Collins, William Phillips, Jean McLeod, June Miller, Les Miller

"The fearful Depression of the thirties has been forgotten... well almost, except by those who still bear its scars and those who are most conscious of the failings of our economic system."
New Theatre leaflet, October 1946

NARRATOR (CONT.)

Moliere's Tartuffe, *a 17th century French farce that ridiculed the hypocrisy of the nobility and the bigotry of the clergy.* Spanish Village, *with a large cast of players and dancers, is a tale of the struggle of the villagers against their overlords, performed here for the first time in Australia.*

New Theatre produced White Justice *a dance musical about the first Aboriginal stockmen's strike in Western Australia of that same year. In 1946 hundreds of Aboriginal pastoral workers walked off stations in the Pilbara region protesting ill treatment and virtual slave conditions. It was made in collaboration with the Australian Aboriginal League.*

They performed JB Priestley's They Came to a City. *In this play nine people of different backgrounds, find themselves mysteriously outside the gates of an idealised city. The characters have to choose this ideal world or their familiar lives. The militant trade unionist carries the editorial; he says he must stay in the old world, so as to fight for a new one available to all.*

The early post-war years in Australia were days of hope. A Labor Government under Chifley promised a new deal in post-war development. Activists organised community campaigns to build child-care centres and libraries.

Trade unions began campaigns to catch up on wages sacrificed during the war. Equality, decent housing, progress and peace seemed to be achievable. Among the Left there was a shared vision of a just future.

For Bob Mathews and Ken Coldicutt, screening films and making films held enormous promise for social change.

An abridged version of *A Place to Live,* this edited version maintains the structure of the original, the passage of its argument, its intertitles and its montage introduced with Ken Coldicutt's recollections. (Music: Carl Vine *Inner World.*)

THE GUARDIAN, October 18, 1946   PAGE SEVEN

New Theatre Play Opens

● A scene from New Theatre's new play "Love On The Dole," which opened last Saturday.

Review

The play deals with the effects of the last depression on a typical small pocket of one of England's industrial areas. Its production is well up to the N.T. standard.

Alf Jones, in his first major part, as young Tommy Hardcastle gives an outstanding performance among the leading characters, but William Phillips in the small part of the local bookmaker's stooge, gives a brilliant character performance.

Chief weakness of the production is its handling of romantic scenes and situations, of which there are more than the usual. The play will run at New Theatre, Flinders Street, until October 30. —B.D.

Support For Rail Workers' Fight

BENDIGO.—A resolution carried at the last meeting of the Bendigo Trades Hall Council endorsed the struggle now being waged by railworkers, and called on all workers to give financial and moral support to the ARU in any further action it might take to secure implementation of its nine-point program.

A similar resolution has been carried by the Bendigo sub-branch of the Fuel and Fodder Union.

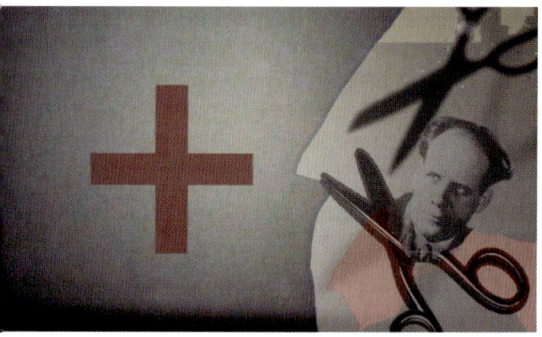

KEN COLDICUTT (V/O)

We very soon got stuck into making a film about Melbourne's housing shortage which was eventually released as a half hour film, A Place to Live.

We'd been through a period of depression with hardly any house building and we'd been through a period of war, altogether, a period of something like 15 years with no working class housing really worth mentioning. So there was a tremendous backlog.

We dealt with the housing shortage, we did a lot of exploration of the inner areas of Fitzroy, Collingwood and South Melbourne and the response of the people was surprising to me. The fact that they weren't a bit afraid to offer themselves and their housing as examples of what was wrong with housing for the workers.

Quite a lot of them are quite happy to invite us into their houses and have a look at the peeling walls, cracked plaster, the rat infested interiors and so forth.

Following observational scenes of slum living conditions in Melbourne's inner city suburbs, the film cuts to exterior shots of the homes of the wealthy. The inter-titles are often ironic and at the same time they issue a demand. We see young children playing in the street, with 'fast cutting' of close traffic; the inter-title: 'Playgrounds for workers children'. We see wealthy holiday homes, empty, and families camping in tents in the bush; the inter-title 'Country homes for the evicted'.

Cut to Bob Mathews.

BOB MATHEWS

Ken was a product of Eisenstein.

Screen design collage and music sequence introducing the figure of Eisenstein, and his montage theory; an image of poverty cut together with an image of wealth, equals the idea inequality; the graphic inter-title: This inequality must end, the workers must own the wealth they produce.

BOB MATHEWS

I was closer to Podovkin really than Eisenstein. I liked movement. The element of movement, camera movement in cinematography fascinated me. That it has the potential for actually producing...

Cut to another individual shot from A Place to Live, in which an emotionally evocative tableau is played out in wide shot.

...a balletic affect, and including what would be editing, in a single shot. I couldn't do it any other way.

Screen design divides the frame in two, a freeze frame of Ken Coldicutt on the left and the Bob Mathews interview on the right – Ken's portrait is replaced with an instance from A Place to Live of very fast cutting of close-ups of traffic, creating a sense of danger for children we have just seen playing in the streets.

BOB MATHEWS

But Ken wanted lots of pieces of film to join together in dramatic effect. However that was a small thing, it didn't affect our friendship.

Bob Mathews' image freezes, and Ken begins to speak, a flash frame presents another collage where screen right is taken up with images illustrating Eisentein's early work.

KEN COLDICOTT

My thinking was governed very strongly by the sort of thinking that Eisenstein was putting forward in the 20s and the early 30s. And a - and a sort of thinking that is made concrete in Strike *and -* Potemkin *and* October.

I think those showed Eisenstein at his peak and showed the real potentialities of film, whereas the films that he made later like Bezhin Meadow *and* Alexander Nevsky *and* Ivan the Terrible, *were films made more or less under duress, where he's forced by the Soviet bureaucracy to make films which were more conventional in their form and to some extent also were more theatrical, than filmic.*

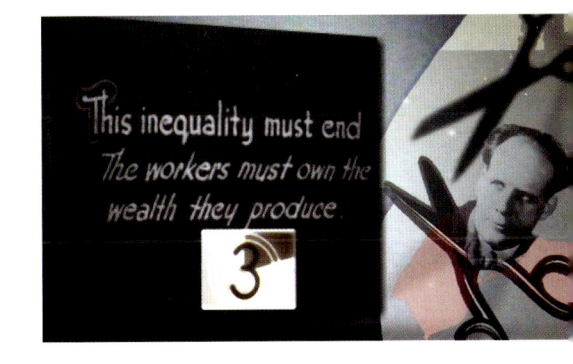

REALIST FILM UNIT,
REALIST FILM UNIT,
REALIST FILM UNIT,

2nd Floor,
330 Flinders Lane,
Melbourne, C.1.
(Telephone: MB2831)

CIRCULAR.

Thursday, February 12, 1948.

Dear Friend,

In our first circular to supporters in 1948, it seems appropriate to summarise our activities in the past year. In this period, we gave 238 public screenings to audiences totalling 31,000 (excluding 126 screenings of a short propaganda film to about 2,400 people at a Community Festival). Organisations covered were as follows:

Young Liberals; Returned Sailors, Soldiers, & Airmen's Imperial League of Australia; Australian Legion of Ex-Servicemen & Women; Australian Labor Party; Australian Communist Party; and various churches.

Screenings were carried out as far away as Mildura, and under the most varied conditions: in public halls, in churches, in private homes; and out-of-doors.

Films screened included: FILM AND REALITY; MEN OF ROCHDALE; THE BRIDGE; CZECHOSLOVAKIA; THE BATTLE FOR THE UKRAINE; INDONESIA CALLING; OUR COUNTRY; METROPOLIS; FAUST; TEN DAYS THAT SHOOK THE WORLD; and a large number of Charlie Chaplin comedies, and other silent revivals.

Films produced included: THE SLUMS ARE STILL WITH US (for the Brotherhood of St. Lawrence); THESE ARE OUR CHILDREN (for the Brotherhood of St. Lawrence); IN MY BEGINNING (for Koornong School); and a newsreel of May Day demonstrations in Sydney, Melbourne, and Adelaide, (For the May Day committee).

In the coming year we aim, with the help of our supporters, to set up a democratic mass organisation interested in using cinema as a force on the side of the people; importing, producing, and exhibiting films, and organising theoretical and practical classes on all aspects of cinema. We would welcome any suggestions you may have as to the name, aims, constitution, and activities of such a body. Even before such an organisation is set up, we intend to organise a short course, to commence next month, for 16mm projectionists. Those wishing to attend are asked to let us know as soon as possible. Another big step has been taken in lodging an order for prints of the classic Soviet silent films. "BATTLESHIP POTEMKIN" is expected to arrive from London in about two months time, and is to be followed by "THE GENERAL LINE", "MOTHER", "THE END OF ST. PETERSBURG", and others.

On the first Sunday in each month this year, we will be screening films at New Theatre in conjunction with Marx School lectures. On Sunday, March 7th, at 7.45pm, films will be screened to illustrate a lecture by Ted Hill on "Science and Religion." Other Sundays at New Theatre will as a rule be devoted entirely to Realist Film Unit screenings.

CHAPTER 3 THE EARLY FILMS: 'REALISM'

Location: Olinda, the home of film historian Graeme Cutts. We see Graeme in his lounge room, with a VHS copy of the Ken Coldicutt interview.

NARRATOR

In the late 1970s film historian Graeme Cutts recorded an interview with Ken. This is the only sound footage ever made of Ken Coldicutt.

Graeme leans toward a monitor, turns up the volume.

GRAEME CUTTS

But here, watch this, this is very nice. This is the garden at Box Hill, the herb garden. This is the beginning. There's me.

Full frame, black and white video, establishing shots of the Graeme Cutts interview with Ken Coldicutt.

NARRATOR

It was shot on a half-inch black and white reel-to-reel video recorder, the Portapak. Then the Portapack was new technology. Its arrival coincided with the counter cultural social movements of the 70s. It provided an affordable technical base for the community-based video movement.

Video-style wipe to Graeme Cutts, on the veranda of his home in Olinda:

GRAEME CUTTS

It was a very convenient medium, it was cheaper than film, and so I went along and arranged an interview with Ken Coldicutt.

Portapak video, soft focus images of Ken Coldicutt obscured by foliage in the garden of Ken's home.

GRAEME CUTTS   (V/O)

I found him very congenial, very urbane. He had a story to tell and he wanted to make sure that people knew the story.

30

Interview with Graeme Cutts:

GRAEME CUTTS

He was very - very sad, almost - well not almost, he was angry about what had happened to him, what had been, - you know whatever the story was with the, - with the Communist Party and…

Series of freeze frames moving closer to a TV monitor in Graeme Cutts' home where the image of Ken Coldicutt is variously framed:

GRAEME CUTTS   (V/O)

…it seemed very acrimonious. There was obviously a ploy to stop the activities of the Realist Film Unit and it, you know, who will ever know whether it was - they didn't like him or they didn't like what he was doing, it's difficult to say. But he was very welcoming to me, because he wanted his story of the Realist Film Unit and the Realist Film Association to be told.

GRAEME CUTTS

Film historian Graeme Cutts taught filmmaking, film history and criticism at Rusden State College (Monash Teachers College). He began his teaching career at Nhill High School in 1962 and quickly became convinced of the potential of the practice and study of cinema in 'progressive' education. His publications include important original work on Australian filmmaker Giorgio Mangiamele and on the Dutch documentary filmmaker Joris Ivens. It was in pursuit of his research on Joris Ivens' Australian film *Indonesia Calling* (1946), that Graeme recorded the only video interview with Ken Coldicutt. The interview was shot around 1978 by a colleague of Graeme's from Rusden, Wolfgang Kress. Graeme is also responsible for locating for preservation the only surviving colour print of the Realists' *In my beginning* (1947), a sponsored film in support of the 'experimental' school 'Koornang' in Warrandyte (1939/47).

Screen Design: A divided frame, Ken Coldicutt left, with on the right slow dissolves through graphic images, *Proletariat*, Communist Party of Australia banner in a march through Melbourne streets…

KEN COLDICUTT

Well in the 30s you would've had to have been pretty buttoned down not to have been very politically aware because this was the time of tremendous unemployment and the growth of fascism overseas, and although I was supposed to be studying science at the university at the time, I became much more concerned about political matters.

The only party that was giving a lead on major issues was the Communist Party, so people who were looking for a lead, and especially a lead on international affairs, naturally, turned towards the Communist Party.

I started university a week after my seventeenth birthday. From that time I would say that I was very politically conscious and thinking a great deal about the possibilities of film as something more than escapist entertainment, something that could be used as a weapon, something that could be used to say something about the political conditions of the time.

Cut to a strip of black and white film and an animated zoom in to one frame.

NARRATOR

The Realists made a film called The Slums Are Still With Us *in 1947. This is now lost. But some fragments from it turned up.*

Tracking shot from a car travelling through Canberra dissolving from black and white to color (narrator with camera in rear vision mirror). Exterior National Film and Sound Archive, Canberra, followed by overlay interior of the National Film and Sound Archive and close-ups from the frames and footage referred to.

NARRATOR

The National Film and Sound Archive had a reel of unidentified trims that had been anonymously deposited years ago. They thought it might be wharfies' footage because it included a shot of a mural with the words 'Waterside Workers'. It included footage of a Peace Congress in Melbourne in 1950, one of the missing Realist films.

We see people collecting signatures for petitions and anti-war graffiti in the early 50s.

I knew the footage was part of the Realist archive because it included off-cuts of shots that appear in their later films.

At the end of the reel a title appears. What followed is fragments and trims from the lost 1947 film, The Slums Are Still With Us. *It evokes social conditions of mid 40s Australia.*

There are shots from scenes of silent scripted drama. We see new experiments with screen design, collage created with super imposition, probably made in the camera by winding the film back and re-exposing the frame.

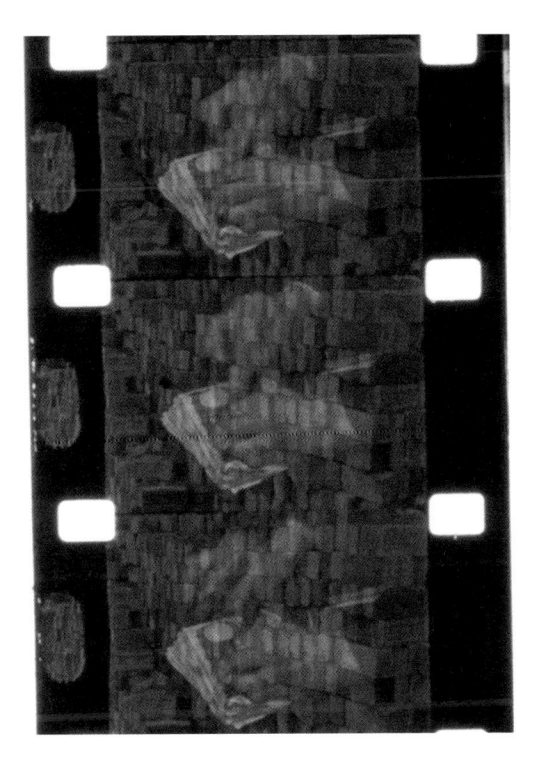

JOHN FLAUS

John Flaus – screen actor, film historian, script editor, radio announcer, film critic, and teacher – has been active in the film society movement since 1953 and published his first film reviews in 1954: he was sacked the same year when he wrote that *On the Waterfront* was right-wing propaganda. He has written widely for film society magazines, *Filmnews*, anarchist journals, metropolitan dailies and more recently online at sensesofcinema.com.

He helped design and set-up the original cinema studies courses at both Sydney and Latrobe Universities in the early 1970s. In the 1980s he started Film Buff's Forecast on 3RRR-FM and formed an unholy radio alliance with Paul Harris, who continues that show 20 years later. As an actor, he has appeared in over 60 feature films and television programs. He has also generously played countless roles in student films. These days he makes a living as an actor, script editor and occasional lecturer. There is a film about Flaus by Melbourne filmmaker Peter Tammer, *The Flaus Film*, (2009).

JOHN FLAUS   (V/O)

What were the Realists doing? They were saying what Kluge and the later generations said, my camera sees what is unseen by the society. Look at the invisible ones.

John Flaus, film historian and scholar, speaks from his home in Castlemaine, rural Victoria.

JOHN FLAUS

I'm very impressed by something that Virginia Woolf wrote in the 20s when she's looking at one of these silent dramas about the privileged caste in England sitting around bemoaning their caste begotten woes of whatever kind they were and there in the background there's a gardener working on a rose bush and Woolf with her peculiar sensitivities says, 'That's what I'm interested in because that's reality'.

Black and white footage from the incomplete *The Slums Are Still With Us* (1947):.

JOHN FLAUS   (V/O)

So realism was, or the champions who were likely to raise a flag called realism and wave it were the ones who were saying, hey it's the everyday, the taken for granted that must be looked at and given a similar degree of attention. This is like, I would suggest, rediscovering childhood. The child who's not familiar with so many of the objects and utensils that are lying around in the home, explores them all, they're all of equal interest.

A doorknob can be a matter of fascination for the child until the child learns that there's a particular social function for that doorknob and after that the child's curiosity disappears, it's discouraged from contemplating the knob in any other way except this one utilitarian function that it has.

Back to John Flaus.

JOHN FLAUS

That's how we lose our innocence as children anyway. You don't have to go to school to have that innocence taken from you, but schools help. So I think this is what the filmmakers…

Black and white scenes from Melbourne city streets, circa 1947 (derived from the trims cases).

JOHN FLAUS   (V/O)

…were saying, there are processes, social processes and political processes that are going on of which we participate only here and there. We see a little of it.

Back to John Flaus.

JOHN FLAUS

During the 1940s Humphrey Jennings made that short little 20-minute film Listen to Britain *which is what I think the Realists in Australia attempted to do; to put into practice what Godard said in the 60s, "If the photograph is truth then film is truth twenty-four times a second."*

A series of black and white shots: a tennis game; close-up: a 'privileged' girl serves a ball / an under-privileged child leaves the front door of an inner city house / a wide shot of girls doubles / a slum dwelling / a 'modern' black of flats /

JOHN FLAUS   (V/O)

…Okay we're looking at grabs, a few seconds here and a few seconds there. Put them together and…

A man's hands light a match, the flame fills the screen.

JOHN FLAUS

…they have another meaning. And yet that other meaning is closer to the whole than the parts themselves could express.

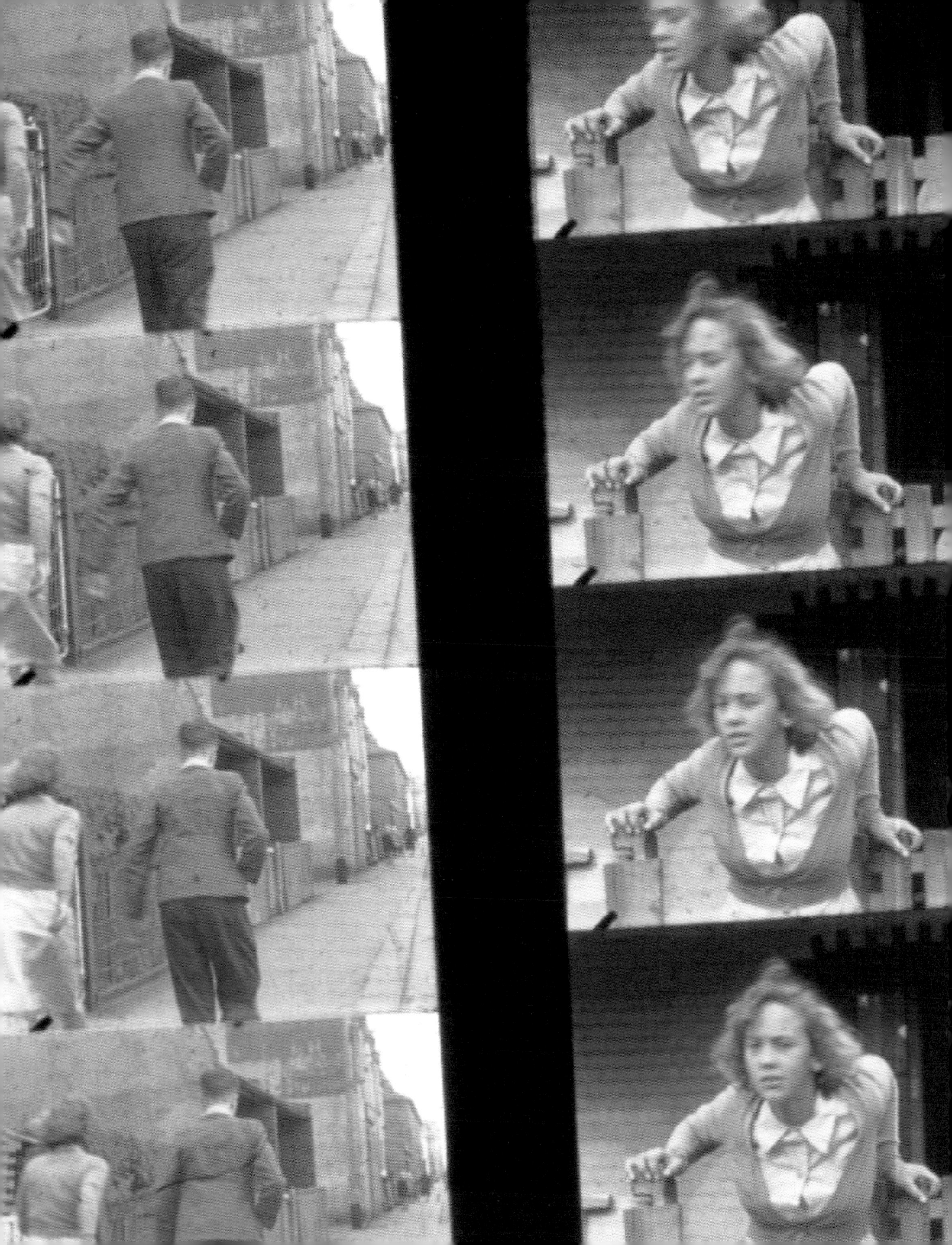

CHAPTER 4 THESE ARE OUR CHILDREN

Joan Pigdon, 2009

JOAN DYSON

Shortly after *The Archive Project* went to air on ABC TV in January 2007 there was an excited telephone call from Joan Pigdon (née Dyson) in Queensland who said a school friend had called her to say that she was that moment watching Joan of 60 years ago on television! (Daylight savings in Victoria, and not in Queensland, meant that Joan had an hour's notice before her scenes were broadcast.) Joan was looking for a copy of the film. She was the 'star' of *These Are Our children*. Later she wrote to me about her recollections. Joan remembered making the film, and the friend who had called her was the only other person who knew about it.

At age 13 Joan was recruited for the part of Molly Bradley by the Brotherhood's Joyce Hay, who was the daughter of a school friend of Joan's mother. Joan said, "They wanted to show Australia - all of us who lived in our lovely leafy suburbs in blissful ignorance, that just a few miles away there was a whole other world full of misery and social injustice." She couldn't recall the name of the boy who plays her brother in the film but she did recall others, "The rest of the family were a real family in Fitzroy, the father worked in a butcher shop and the mother suffered from rheumatoid arthritis… They had, I think, seven children… The children slept three or four to a bed." Joan described living conditions that shocked her at the time and how as a result she was motivated to support the Brotherhood's work: "I have never forgotten that family or the other families I met with Joyce, or the dark, terrible houses and conditions." Joan recalls that Joyce Hay plays the associate of the Magistrate in the Childrens' Court scene. "I'm quite sure it was my experience with the Brotherhood and the wonderful work they do, the families in so much need and Joyce, who was an absolute inspiration, that made me choose nursing as my career."

Joan Dyson's background was at the opposite end of the spectrum to the part she played as Molly; her brothers were at Melbourne Grammar and she went to Firbank. The family lived in Brighton. Their experience was more like that depicted in the closing scenes of *These Are Our Children*, where we see young people enjoying tennis, park lands and the sports facilities of the privileged schools. "I used to take the train to Flinders Street Station and go past Richmond and think absently in passing; 'Oh, that's where the poor people live', without a clue in the world… Well, what a rude awakening I had and what a profound affect it had." (February 23, 2007)

Colour, close-up as a young man's hands thread a 16mm camera (*Film-Work*); frames from *These Are Our Children* are animated against the action (checking for scratches).

JOHN FLAUS   (V/O)

You're never going to be able to photograph everything. The first necessary – you know the origins of things are – you decide to shoot something.

Title: black and white *These Are Our Children*; an edited version of the film following the structure of the original. *These Are Our Children* was a silent film. Music here is Carl Vine *Inner World*.

KEN COLDICUTT   (V/O)

The Brotherhood of St Laurence sponsored a film called These Are Our Children *which was an account of the lives and the reasons for delinquency of the children growing up in the inner suburbs.*

Screen design setting John Flaus as an element alongside the elements of the film he analyses.

JOHN FLAUS

These Are Our Children has a very interesting narrative structure because even works of fiction at this time, though quite a few of them would start on that basis of having arrived at what was almost the end of the story then what you will get is the body of the work which is explaining where we were and at the end we're brought back to where we started.

And even with fiction at that time it would be obligatory to supply the resolution that the material is crying out for. So the work has to carry a solution for the problem that it examined. And certainly films had to do this. Didn't happen.

So this would be one of the earliest examples that I know in film history of an audience being required to actually have to take away with them, the entire body of the work and then in their own minds arrive at the solution they wanted.

THESE ARE OUR CHILDREN
DVD COMMENTARY TRACK BY JOHN MURPHY

John Murphy: The Brotherhood had moved to Fitzroy in 1933, into a very poor working class area in the middle of the Depression. The Brotherhood was a tiny organisation at that stage: so the films belong to a quite early period when the Brotherhood had been there in Fitzroy for 14, 15 years. It's a very small organisation that's really built around the charismatic figure of Gerard Tucker himself.

Tucker was relatively unsophisticated, very much an action man. You know, you'd see a problem and you'd think about a solution to it. He's very good at starting something and grabbing good people to work on it. "We've got to do something about these slums", and he'd go and knock on doors. "Governments are doing nothing because they believe that people are indifferent; we've got to mobilise the people out of their indifference and get films made and approach the Premier and demand action" and so forth.

In 1936 the Housing Investigation and Slum Abolition Board had 6,000 houses within a five kilometre radius of the GPO listed as seriously substandard; 6,000 houses multiplied by ten, 60,000 people within five miles of the GPO, rented accommodation, slum landlords […] It just gets worse and worse, in suburbs from Port Melbourne to Richmond to Collingwood, Fitzroy, some in Carlton. They never advocated tower blocks, and they were pretty horrified when they started going up. It's one of the real ironies of the Brotherhood's activism that the solution to the problem they demanded must be solved, is then seen as the new problem that they've got to deal with, which is the conditions of people living in Housing Commission high-rise flats.

By the end of the war you've got such a severe housing shortage in Australia, shortage of materials, a baby boom that's been going on since the start of the 40s. The Housing Commissions actually doesn't do anything about slums, it builds outer suburban housing, a huge amount of outer suburban housing […] What's brutalising children and youth – for people like Tucker – is living in conditions which are brutalising. The social category of the delinquent is to a large extent born around the same time as the social category of the teenager, this new social phenomenon of those on a cusp between childhood and adulthood. And so the social problem of delinquency, the public talk about delinquency, really belongs more to the mid 1950s.

How you can help the B.S.L. in its war against slums and all the evils that come therefrom.

You might perhaps take a 5/- collecting card. You could get one before you leave the hall tonight.

He toured these films around the suburbs and then he toured them around country Victoria. He had a driver who drove him around with a caravan on the back and they took a projector with him, and they'd go to country towns and camp the caravan in the local churchyard, set up the projector in a hall and show the film. Tucker would do the commentary, so he was narrating as the silent films were running. Tucker talked about the poorer health of kids in the slums compared to kids in the wealthier suburbs, the inequality of society. He saw that as injustice. He was a small 'l' liberal. He'd come out of a conservative social justice tradition. The filmmakers themselves have come from a more articulate, radical position.

The worry about cinema and comics as influences is actually a more conservative high-culture kind of anxiety; that the culture is being debased by comics […] The Communist Party and other radical movements had a quite sophisticated sense of culture; I think it's surprising that comics and film appear as part of the narrative, but maybe it is a nationalist thing.

The whole slum genre does have a major problem in it; it's an observation from outside that has virtually no idea that there's a community there. It's a double-edged sword really. It's necessary to mobilise this sense of outrage from richer suburbs in order to get any policy action, but in doing so […] most of the advocates for action on the slums actually end up also ignoring the nature of the community that lives there.

Tucker had this idea of establishing a group of priests and laypeople who would be temporarily attached to the Brotherhood which would live ascetically, but live in the world and do social action. It never came to anything; he didn't actually get to build this order called the Brotherhood. What he got to build was a major welfare organisation that's been at the forefront since the 50s really of social action campaigns, research, policy advocacy. It's a major institution in Melbourne.

50 YEARS OF MOVIES!

REALIST FILM UNIT Presents:

Film & Reality

Sequences from 58 Films!

NEWSREEL, DOCUMENTARY FEATURE!
French, German, Soviet, Dutch, British, American!

"The Great Train Robery"
"Nanook of the North"
"The Covered Wagon"
"Battleship Potemkin"
"The General Line"
"Turksib"
"Kameradschaft"
"Life of Emile Zola"
"La Grande Illusion"

A History of the Realist Film Compiled by CAVALCANTI and LINDGREN for the British Film Institute

Screening at NEW THEATRE
92 FLINDERS ST., CITY

FOUR NIGHTS ONLY! Don't Miss it!
EASTER SAT., SUN., MON. and TUES.
March 27th, 28th, 29th and 30th, at 8

No Admission Charge, but Donations Accepted

REALIST FILM UNIT, 330 Flinders Lane, C.1.   MB 2831

CHAPTER 5 SCREENINGS

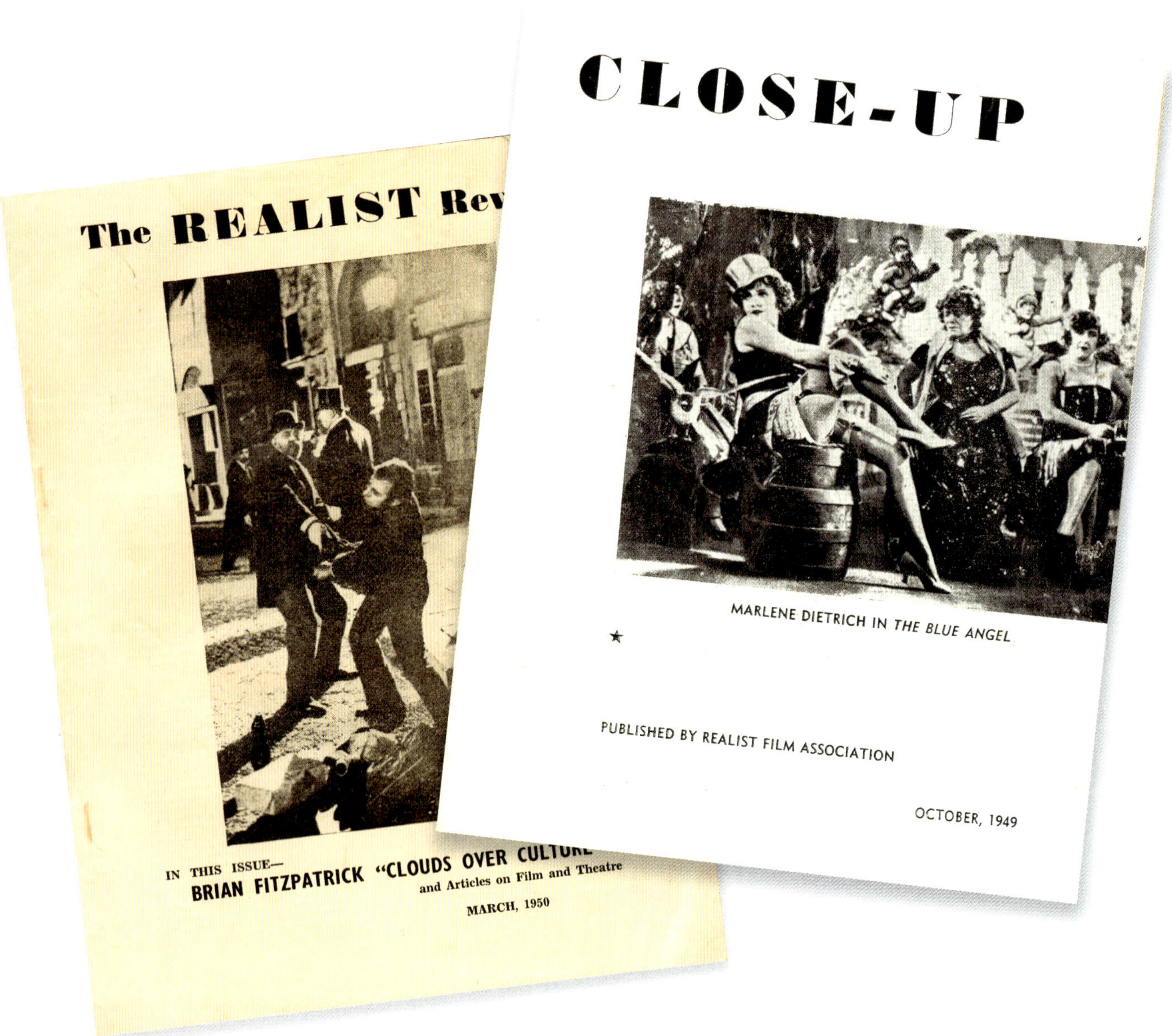

CLOSE-UP

MARLENE DIETRICH IN *THE BLUE ANGEL*

PUBLISHED BY REALIST FILM ASSOCIATION

OCTOBER, 1949

The REALIST Review

IN THIS ISSUE—
BRIAN FITZPATRICK "CLOUDS OVER CULTURE"
and Articles on Film and Theatre

MARCH, 1950

REALIST FILM News
Realist Film Association, 92 Flinders St., Melbourne

Realist Film News was published monthly (circa October 1950 – March 1958), with *Close-up* (October 1949) and *The Realist Review* (March 1950) each having only one edition. There were plans on occasion to combine these publications with the Melbourne New Theatre's *New Theatre Review*, but the film screenings and the theatre performances tended to operate independently. The State Library of Victoria holds an almost complete series of *Realist Film News*.

A montage of still images evoking the machinery of editing.

KEN COLDICUTT   (V/O)

These Are Our Children was edited in a hell of a rush. I spent a week working at night, I had no other time to work, and I didn't even see the first screening of it, because I was already occupied doing the screenings at the New Theatre at the weekend.

Screen design; a projector lens on frame left as Bob Mathews speaks screen right (the Deane Williams interview).

BOB MATHEWS   (V/O)

Ken was absolutely in love with films and showing films, and every time I believe every time he showed a film, he enjoyed it again with the audience.

Overlay footage of projectors rolling, dissolve to a still of Gerry Harant behind a projector at an early Melbourne Film Festival.

We built a projection box and Ken began giving lessons in film projection, which drew more people. Possibly Gerry Harant would have been the first because Gerry was working in the theatre. He was doing technical work in the theatre, lighting and sound and so on. So Gerry would have been part of the projection side.

Dissolve from the still of Gerry Harant to Harant interview, 3CR Community Radio, Melbourne.

GERRY HARANT

Students in particular had read about all these films and you couldn't see them because there was no public screening. So ultimately if they wanted to see these films they could only see them in our public screening.

"THERE WAS NO VENUE AT ALL SHOWING AUSTRALIAN DOCUMENTARIES..."

GERRY HARANT

Gerhart (Gerry) Harant was born in Austria and came to Australia a refugee from fascism in 1939. He worked in industry from the age of 16 in jobs ranging from process work to research and development. Gerry was active in the New Theatre, Realist Film Unit and Association, and the Melbourne Film Festival. He was a member of the Communist Party for many years, and is the longest serving member of the Melbourne Film Festival. For much of the Festival's life Gerry was in charge of film projection.

He has worked as a volunteer with community radio over a number of decades, making programs, broadcasting, and contributing articles to *Overland* magazine. The National Archives of Australia, the National Film and Sound Archive and the Oral History Collection of the National Library of Australia hold records. He is co-author with Ken Coldicutt and Joan Coxsedge, *Rooted In Secrecy*, CAPP, Melbourne, 1982.

REALIST FILM UNIT

Circular.

2nd Floor,
330 Flinders Lane,
MELBOURNE, C.1.
Phone: Central 3711.

OUR FIRST YEAR.

January, 1947.

Formed towards the end of 1945, the Realist Film Unit recently concluded its first year of activity. A non-profit organisation, operating on a small capital subscribed by working members, the Unit fulfilled three important functions:-

1. A REPERTORY CINEMA: The Unit has helped to develop intelligent appreciation of the youngest of the arts by screening revivals as well as important current productions which are denied commercial release. In 1946: The Unit organised a number of city screenings, mainly at New Theatre; silent films shown included: "CRAINQUEBILLE"; "GRASS"; "TEN DAYS THAT SHOOK THE WORLD"; "THE WHITE HELL OF PITZ PALU"; "METROPOLIS"; and many of the early Chaplin and Mack Sennett comedies. Sound films included: the Soviet productions: "69th PARALLEL"; "NO GREATER LOVE"; "SPRING SONG"; the American documentaries: "THE VALLEY OF THE TENNESSEE"; "THE CITY"; "A BETTER TOMORROW"; "FIGHTING LADY"; the British-American war-documentary "THE TRUE GLORY"; the British documentaries: "WORLD OF PLENTY"; "NORTH SEA"; "BORDER WEAVE"; the French feature-films "THREE WALTZES" and "LA KERMESSE HEROIQUE"; Canadian National Film Board productions; and documentaries from China, Czechoslovakia, and Yugoslavia.

The Unit was responsible for the recovery from the Commonwealth Investigation Branch of the documentary on the Chinese Red Army, "CHINA STRIKES BACK"; and we broke the (unofficial) ban by Victorian exhibitors on "INDONESIA CALLING" by purchasing a print of the film and organising public screenings.

2. NON-THEATRICAL SHOWS: From the proceeds of city screenings the Unit has provided a much-needed projection service at unusually low prices for working-class and cultural organisations. In 1946: 215 shows were given to audiences totalling 21,000. Increasing demand for the Unit's services is shown by the fact that over half of these shows took place in the last three months of the year. Organisations assisted in this way included: Schools; youth clubs; trade unions; community centres. Shows were given in public halls, schools, churches, club-rooms, private homes, and even out-of-doors. Not only Melbourne and suburbs were covered, but also Geelong, Ballarat, Healesville, Yarra Junction, Yarram, Sale, Mirboo, Foster, Maffra, and Wonthaggi.

3. FILM PRODUCTION: The Unit has also proved that film production need not remain the close preserve of the big financial interests, but that films can be made to serve the interests of the people. Newsreels have been taken of workers' demonstrations and strike struggles. Short films were made of all New Theatre stage productions in 1946. The color film "400 FILM STARS", showed how young workers of the Eureka Youth League organise their own holiday camp. "YOUTH PLANS ITS FUTURE" dealt with the campaign for the improvement of young workers and apprentices in Victoria. "A PLACE TO LIVE", vividly revealing the extent of Melbourne's housing crisis, was an example of the way in which films can be used to tackle important social problems in Australia.

In 1947: The Realist Film Unit will greatly increase its production activities. Already in production is a color film about Australia's outstanding progressive school, "Koornong", and next on the list is a film explaining the trade union attitude to wages and prices.

The Realists published detailed Annual Reports during the first years of their operation. The Realist Film Unit became incorporated into the Realist Film Association in 1948 when Ken Coldicutt, Bob Mathews, Gerry Harant and others decided that they could more effectively build the exhibition aspect of their work if they opened up the organisation to a membership (a 'democratic mass organisation' in the jargon of the day). Annual Reports and other internal documents after 1952 are missing, possibly destroyed around the time when the records were moved to the Queensbury Street offices of the Eureka Youth League in the late 1950s.

Overlay, animated screen design illustrating from documents the diversity of films and the countries from which they derived.

GERRY HARANT

It was one of the points in our constitution, that we should counteract the workings of the Hollywood film. It was very much the policy that underlay our activities because we were screening films that related to that ultimate objective.

We were absolutely appalled by the fact that at that particular time there was only a single theatre, or sometimes two showing European cinema and early Australian cinema. And there was no venue at all showing Australian documentaries.

We felt that it was up to a non-commercial outfit to remedy this situation. Of course we were all members of the Communist Party.

We did treat what we were doing as a Left involvement.

So basically it was a shared involvement between politics and I suppose the artistic side that motivated us.

FORBIDDEN FILMS . . .

"MILLIONS OF US."

REALIST FILM ASSOCIATION POLICY

The policy of the Realist Film Association is to develop the use of films as a force for social progress, as a weapon in the struggle for peace and socialism. Our policy is carried out in the following ways:

By showing films which are boycotted from commercial screens of Australia – films which deal honestly with the living conditions and needs of the Australian people, films which tell the truth about socialism;

By importing from the Soviet Union, China, and the People's Democracies of Eastern Europe films which would otherwise never be seen in Australia;

By showing films of outstanding artistic and historic interest which the general public is not otherwise able to see;

By producing films dealing with the problems of the Australian people;

By opposing those who regard films merely as profit-making commodities or as a means of spreading reactionary propaganda and escapist illusions.

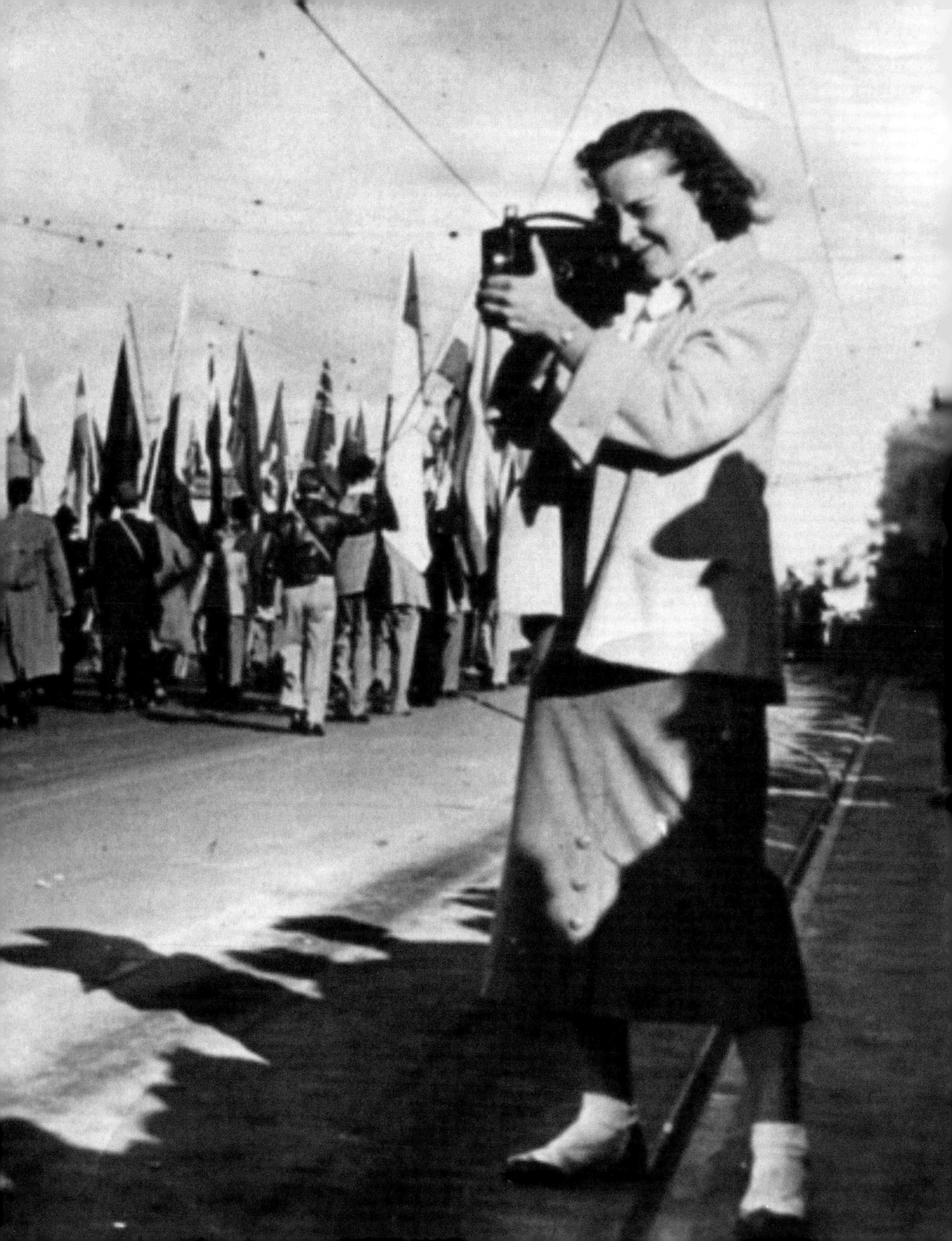

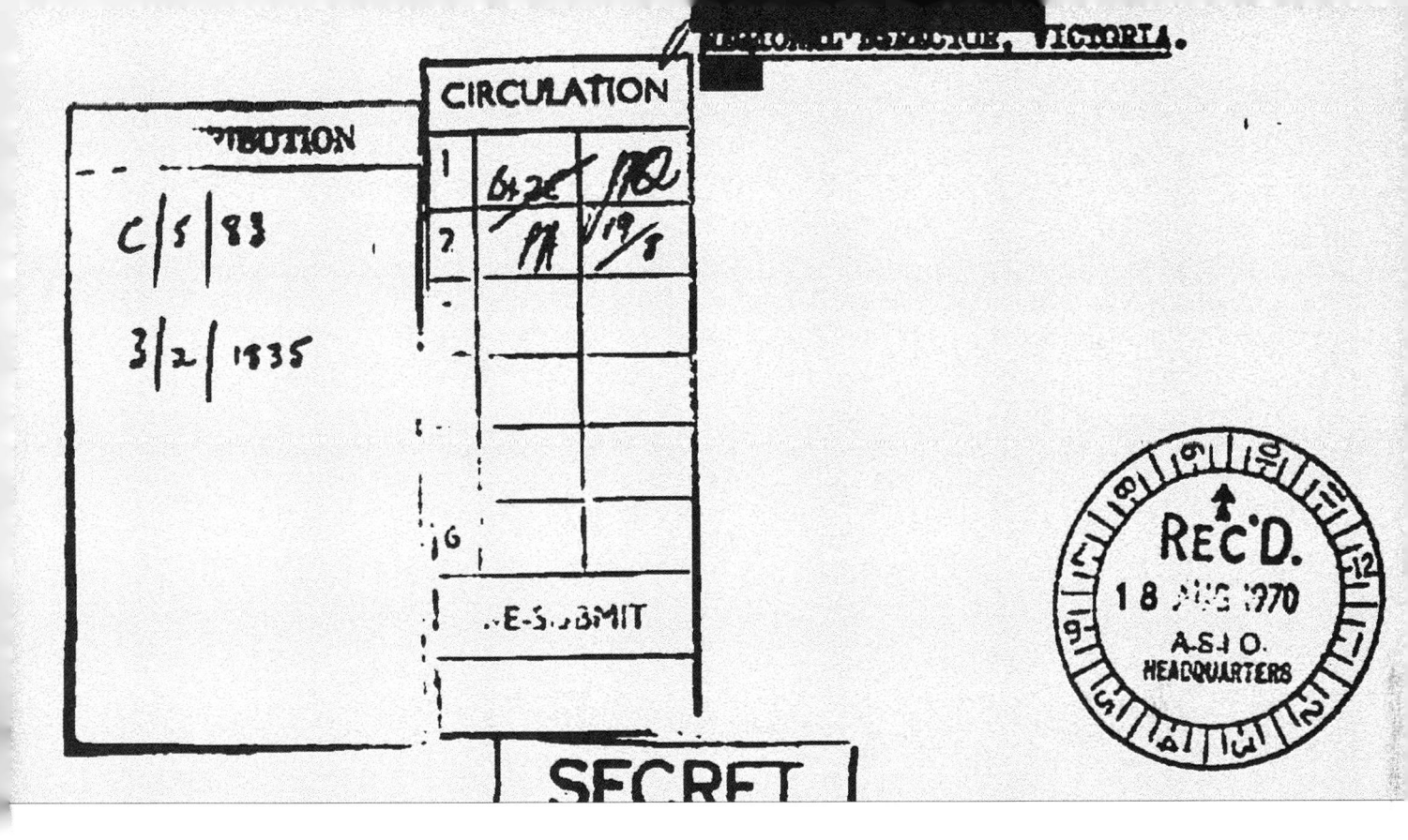

CHAPTER 6 ADVERSELY KNOWN

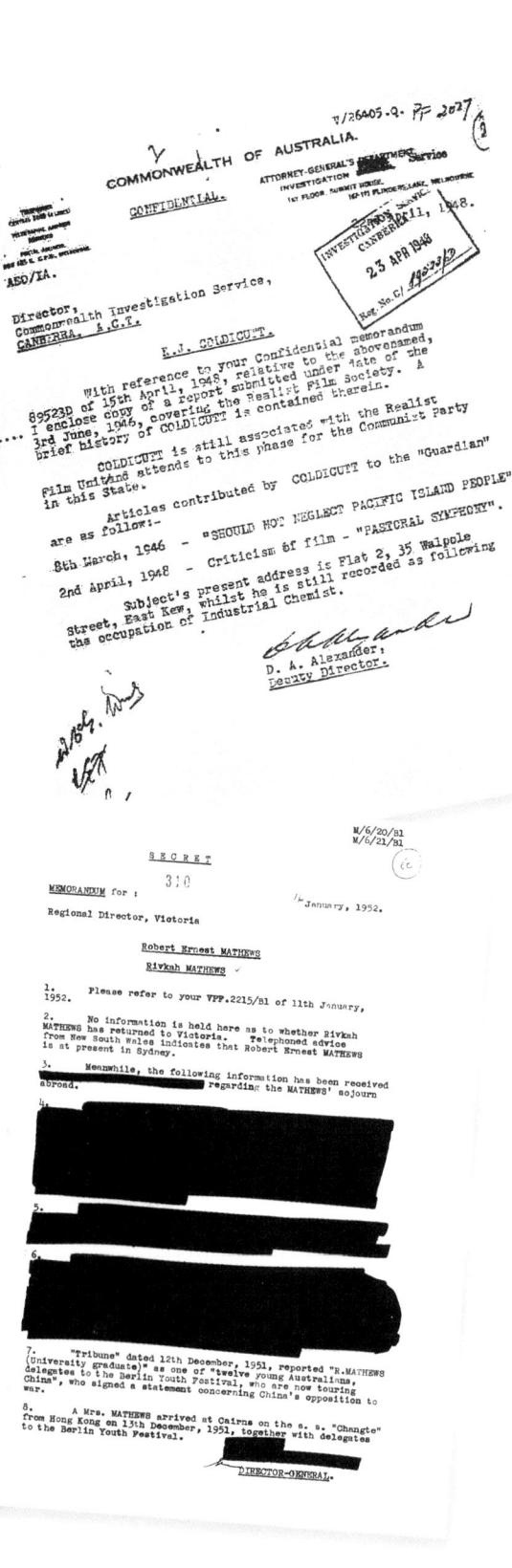

Overlay, animated screen design with Commonwealth Investigation Service documents illustrating the following narration:

NARRATOR

Within months of the Realist Film Unit being established, secret dossiers were being exchanged between the Victorian Police Special Branch and the Commonwealth Investigation Service. Bob Mathews and Ken Coldicutt had been 'adversely known' and watched by the security organisations for years.

Their cultural work in film and theatre was imagined by security to be a function of the Communist Party, rather than that their involvement with the Party and their dedication to film culture were part of their broad commitment to social change. The Cold War was beginning to build and for the Security Services the Communist Party was the principle enemy.

V/O
(QUOTES DOCUMENTS)

"Coldicutt was born on the 23rd of March 1915. He is still associated with the Realist Film Unit and attends to this phase for the Communist Party in this state."

"Mathews was born on the 22nd of May 1911."

"Coldicutt was film organiser for the friends of the Soviet Union and organizing secretary of the Spanish…"

"Mathews was associated with the anti-war movement. While no evidence is held that he is a member of the Communist Party it is confidently believed that he is imbued with at least Communist ideals."

Cut to: Elizabeth Coldicutt in her inner city apartment:

ELIZABETH COLDICUTT

Sounds like awful paranoia but in a group of 10 or 12 effectively working left-wingers, you can be sure there's someone watching.

50

NARRATOR

Elizabeth Coldicutt first met Ken as an undergraduate when she took part in a conversation in the cafeteria at Melbourne University that led to the formation of the Melbourne University Film Society.

ELIZABETH COLDICUTT

Well coffee's up.

Overlay, slow move on a photograph of Elizabeth Coldicutt at the Olinda Film Festival, 1952.

NARRATOR

At Ken's suggestion she applied for the job of librarian at the State Film Centre. She was responsible for importing films that were screened by the growing film society movement and in no time she was caught up in the cultural Cold War. While she was working at the State Film Centre, she became active with the Melbourne Realists.

Dissolve to a photograph of Elizabeth shooting footage of a May Day March, Melbourne, 1950 (still: David Muir).

ELIZABETH COLDICUTT (V/O)

The screenings had a shape. They would nearly always have some sort of cartoon or puppet film to start. There were wonderful puppet films from Czechoslovakia that we could just borrow from the consulate which was in Sydney, so there were always hair-raising situations about whether the film would arrive in time.

Rapid bursts down to the railway station to pick up the films.

And then there would be something else a little longer, maybe a two-reeler of some kind, a documentary from wherever.

Then there'd be an interval and then when the audience was reseated, Coldicutt would give them a burst about the film and at the same time probably commenting on the political situation of the day. Our audience was already a left-wing audience on the whole and those who had dared

"...YOU CAN BE SURE THERE'S SOMEONE WATCHING."

ELIZABETH COLDICUTT

Elizabeth was a student at Melbourne University in the early post-war years, where she was one of the founders of the Melbourne University Film Society. During the war Elizabeth worked as a radar technician, army driver and teacher. She saw *Prices and the People* (RFU, 1948) at a May Day screening and committed herself to the work of the Realist Film movement. As Film Librarian with the State Film Centre she recommended films for acquisition, organised screenings and touring exhibitions throughout Victoria and wrote for *Film Monthly* and *Film Guide*.

She worked with the Realist Film Association on screenings, publicity and forums. She also contributed as a cinematographer and editor on the Realists' documentation projects. Later, she returned to a teaching career at Sunshine, Preston, Brunswick and Collingwood Technical Schools. She was active in the Technical Teacher's Union until her retirement in 1989. Elizabeth didn't stop work. She continues to contribute to projects in support of refugees, and for equitable housing.

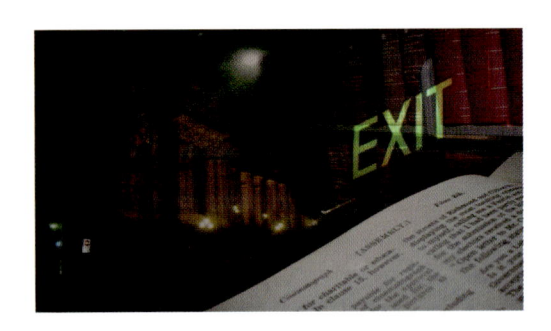

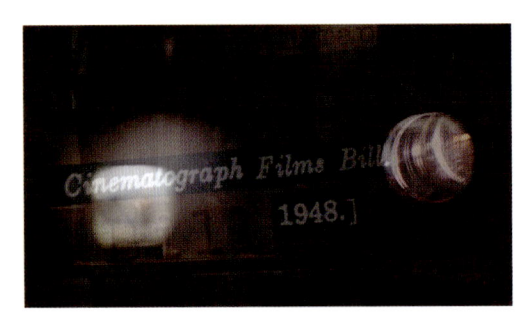

to come into this hotbed of communism, the New Theatre, they listened. And they came really for the film.

But the film itself, when I say 'the film', the main feature film, which was a classic from some historic period in cinema history, that was something that would've had some residual affect in everyone's mind I think, because they're such strong works.

Overlay screen design montage illustrating the screenings and introducing the Cinematograph Bill (1948).

KEN COLDICUTT   (V/O)

In 1948 we reached a total of 305 screenings throughout Victoria and these were very largely to organisations which had no connection with the Communist Party at all. We were working – working at a hell of a rate.

NARRATOR

A campaign against the Realists was launched in the Victorian Parliament when a Bill was introduced designed to restrict film society screenings.

KEN COLDICUTT   (V/O)

It was directed in the first instance at the Realist Film Association, and the best evidence of that was a statement from Mr Cremean himself: 'It may, that is the Bill, may, and I hope it will, be a check on the activities of the Realist Film Unit, which up till now has played merry hell with its propaganda exhibitions.'

NARRATOR

The Cinematograph Films Bill redefined the meaning of theatre, requiring the registration of any place where films were screened and a collection was taken up.

Cut to Gerry Harant interview:

GERRY HARANT

Although the initial object of the Bill was to get at the Realist Film Unit, in fact the provisions were such as to attack every organisation, every non-commercial organisation that was making use of film exhibitions. Churches would have had to register, as well as schools, you know. They found it extremely difficult to find anybody to draft a sort of document that would separate the kosher activities from the non-kosher ones.

They had speeches in the House, usual wild accusations. If you were a Communist you didn't actually find out how good you were until you read some of the things that you were accused of.

Animated graphic, a State Film Centre graphic circa 1950, still photograph Elizabeth Coldicutt working on an exhibition of film posters for the Melbourne Film Festival, 1953.

NARRATOR

At the same time the State Film Centre came under attack for certain films that Elizabeth had imported. The State Film Centre was the primary source of documentary films for churches, schools and community organisations, and Elizabeth was well placed to assist in the campaign against the Bill.

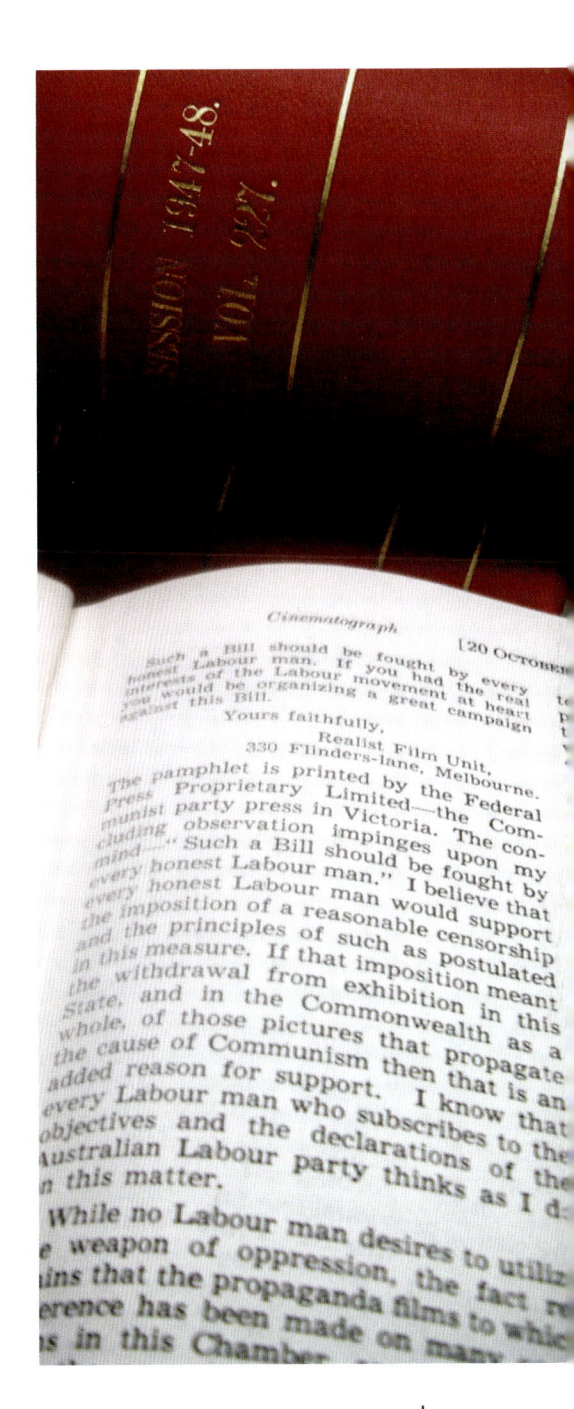

ELIZABETH COLDICUTT (V/O)

I was able to get the addresses…

Elizabeth Coldicutt interview:

ELIZABETH COLDICUTT

…of borrowers of films from the State Film Centre who would be affected by the Cinematographic Films Bill. You can't run a political campaign without some sort of mailing list. And it was ready-made there at the State Film Centre.

And I lost my job because of that, because I was after hours standing at the filing cabinet writing the names and addresses of borrowers from the State Film Centre and Neil Edwards my boss was outraged. He came and found me at this filing cabinet, asked me what I was doing and I told him, I was so naive. I said "I'm just copying out names and addresses of borrowers to tell them about the Cinematographic Films Bill". "Oh you can't do that, that's confidential" or whatever. I believe I said – my memory is that I said "Oh don't be a chicken Neil, this is in the public interest". Didn't cut too well coming from a 20-year-old.

Graphic montage of documents:

KEN COLDICUTT (V/O)

There was really no opposition until we started our campaign, the signing of petitions against the Bill. Part of the campaign was the organisation of a big meeting in Unity Hall and it led to a procession through the streets of Melbourne and eventually to the virtual defeat of the Bill.

THE STATE FILM CENTRE

The State Film Centre was established in Victoria in 1946. State Film Centres were established around Australia as a result of lobbying by documentary film culture activists. The State Film Centres built up libraries of 16mm prints of films from around the world, often under the slogan 'Films With a Purpose'. Along with the National Library in Canberra, they serviced film societies with an interest in film culture, and also community groups, churches and schools with a wide range of programs and inituitives. In Victoria the State Film Centre and its collection became the basis of a new organisation and practice ACMI (Australian Centre for the Moving Image) in the mid 1990s.

When Elizabeth Coldicutt left her job at the State Film Centre in 1948, her position was filled by two men, one of whom, Ed. 'Scheff' Schefferle managed the State Film Centre, advised the Melbourne Film Festival and generally supported local and international, educational film culture with dedication and enthusiasm until his retirement. He still runs film societies today with enormous optimism and love of film and film culture.

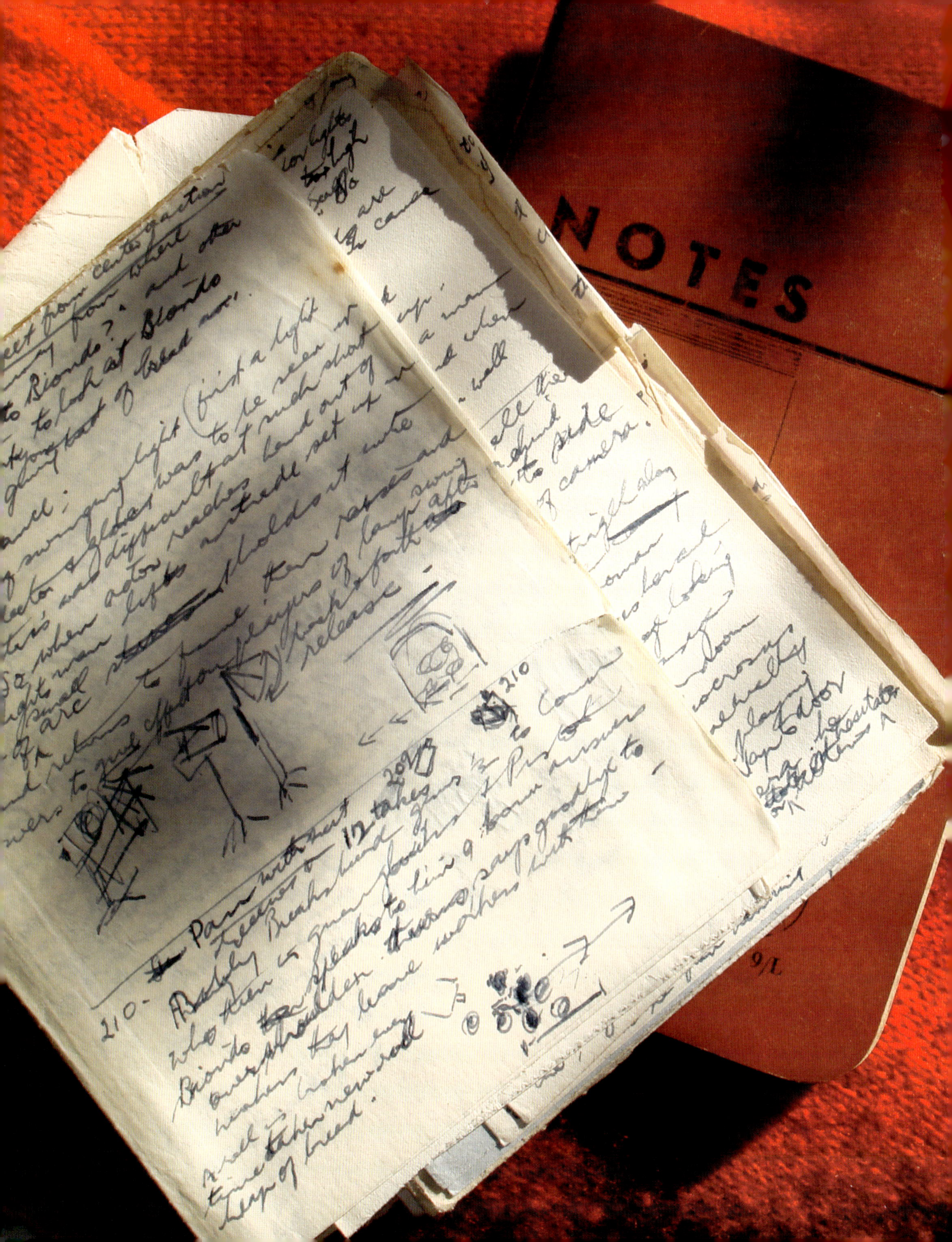
NOTES

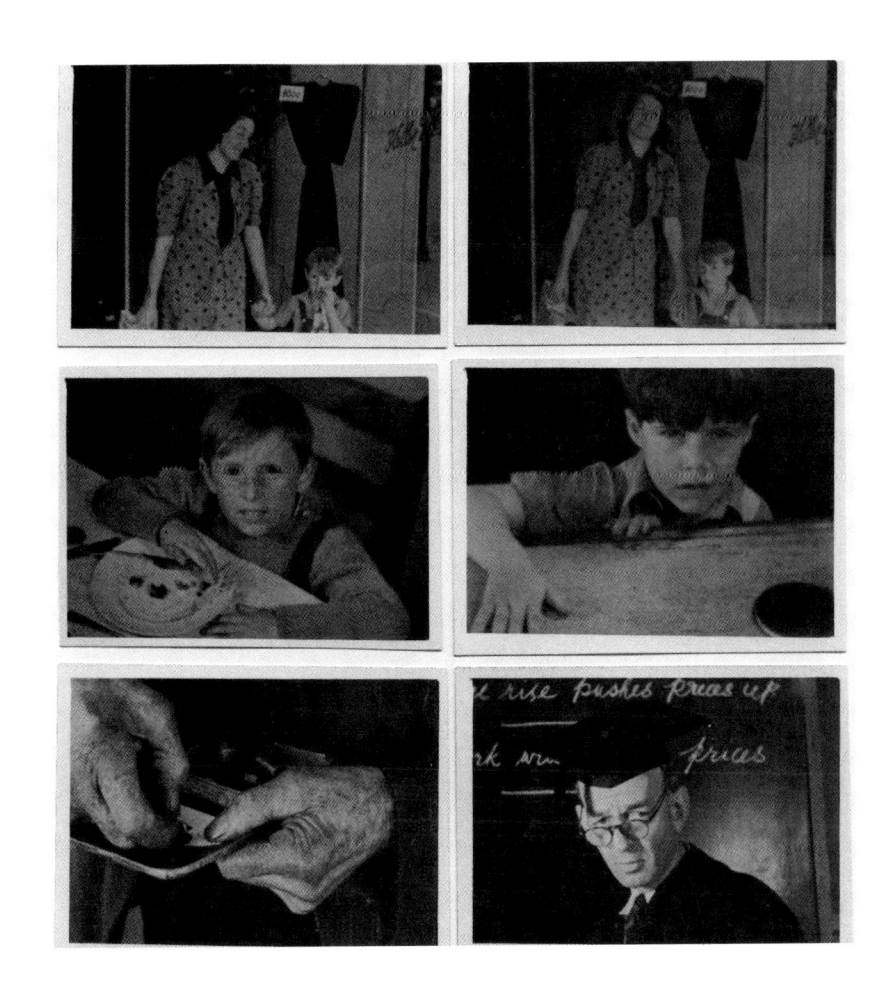

CHAPTER 7 PRICES AND THE PEOPLE

Location: Huzzah Sound, Moore Park, NSW, Louise Smith, Mark Rogers, Nico Lathouris and Bryan Brown are recording 'post-sync' dialogue effects and re-voiced commentary for *Prices and the People* (1948).

LOUISE SMITH   SYNC

Sixpence for that. Hello, what do you think that is.

MARK ROGERS   (V/O)

Four and a half bob, that's robbery, daylight robbery.

BRYAN BROWN   (V/O)

He sells to the wholesaler at four pounds…

BRYAN BROWN

…four, who sells to the retailer at four pounds sixteen, who sells to you at six pounds fifteen.

Throughout this sequence we cut between the original *Prices and the People* soundtrack and the new re-voiced version, with its added post-sync dialogue, sync-effects and atmosphere tracks. The original film has no synchronous dialogue.

BRYAN BROWN

Everyone here can help to bring this about.

ORIGINAL NARRATOR

Everyone here can help to bring this about.

NARRATOR

The only surviving print of Prices and the People *has a very damaged soundtrack. I decided we should build a new soundtrack with atmosphere and effects tracks and re-recorded narration, to make the film more accessible.*

ORIGINAL NARRATOR

Support union action to curb prices and force up wages.

Prices and the People: Interior Butcher shop (recreated dialogue).

Top: Louise Smith, Nico Lathouris.
Middle: Mark Rogers.
Bottom: Bryan Brown.
Huzzah Sound, Sydney, February 2004

BUTCHER

Yes madam?

CUSTOMER

How much is that?

BUTCHER

A very nice cut of meat, one pound ten. Lamb chops, ten and six.

CUSTOMER

That's too much.

BUTCHER

What about a leg of lamb?

CUSTOMER

No, can I have a pound of mince please.

Prices and the People: Interior lolly shop.

SHOP KEEPER (O/S)

What is it lad?

YOUNG BOY (O/S)

Can I have a chocolate frog please?

CU: the shopkeeper's hand pushes a chocolate frog toward the boy. The boy offers his coin. The man takes back the chocolate.

SHOP KEEPER

Sorry sonny, they've gone up.

A woman shopper in a greengrocer's store holds a stick of limp celery.

CUSTOMER

How much?

SHOP KEEPER

Sixpence madam.

CUSTOMER

Sixpence? For that? Oh, it's robbery!

"SORRY SONNY, THEY'VE GONE UP"

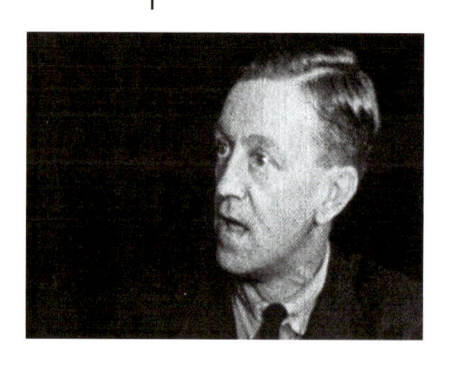

"FOUR AND HALF BOB, THAT'S ROBBERY, DAYLIGHT ROBBERY!"

A man sitting in a restaurant has just finished his meal. A waitress delivers the bill.

WAITRESS (O/S)

There you go.

CUSTOMER

Thank you. What? Four and half bob, that's robbery, daylight robbery!

NARRATOR

Prices and the People *was very difficult to finance. Eventually the Communist Party decided that they would sponsor the film. It was to be an advocacy film for a 'Yes' vote during the 1948 referendum on Commonwealth control of prices and rents.*

P & P NARRATOR (BRYAN BROWN)

They realise that the unceasing stream of price increases wipes out wage gains won by powerful unions after bitter struggles. These battles were fought to bring wages closer – (cut off)…

Cut to: Melbourne stop work meeting occupying the city, June 2005, with huge crowds, banners, 'Protect Worker's Rights'. We see young people selling the newspaper *Green Left*. A Union Representative, Bryan Boyd, Victorian Trades Hall Council, is being interviewed by a TV crew.

BRYAN BOYD

Yes basically up until now you can have at least 20 or 30 matters in a collective agreement through the Australian Industrial Relations Commission.

What Howard's going to do is say only five issues can be in an agreement now. That's all. Wages, hours of work, time in lieu and maternity leave, something like that. Four or five issues. Everything else can be imposed on you by the employer and you've got no recourse to any independent umpire.

60

Cut back to *Prices and the People*: An elderly man takes tobacco from a tin and, with shaking hands, rolls a cigarette. We see his tobacco tin is nearly empty, with butts, saved for another occasion.

P & P NARRATOR (BRYAN BROWN)

Here's one of the most helpless victims of inflated prices. The old age pensioner. Those hands helped to build this country, its roads, its homes, its towns, its vital industries and after a lifetime of hard work he gets 42 and sixpence a week to live on.

Old age means leisure, warmth, the right kinds of food and at least a few comforts.

Prices and the People: The elderly man places a paper bag on his kitchen table. He butts out his hand-rolled cigarette into the tin, and saves the butt. A close up shows the newspaper headline "Tobacco Co's Profit rises to £120,7282".

Two eggs at three pence each? Must be pension day. Save that butt old timer, tobacco's one and six an ounce. That's what the price people think necessary to yield a fair profit to the tobacco monopoly.

Screen design: a series of stills from *Prices and the People* arranged as a scrapbook, with a still of Ken Coldicutt. Animation introduces a screen within the frame on which we see further scenes from *Prices and the People*; a woman is doling out sausages to a family of children. The little boy we saw refused a chocolate frog in an earlier scene here reaches for an extra sausage, but is not allowed it. A close-up holds the questioning expression of the child.

KEN COLDICUTT   (V/O)

Now we first had the idea of Prices and the People back in 1946 with the beginnings of post war inflation, which continued. You had a recurrence of the old cry that 'you mustn't give the workers any more wages because that only increases prices'. And we wanted to make a film which would provide the trade unions with an answer to this sort of nonsense. In other words we wanted to incorporate in film, if you like…

Screen design: an animation moves across a printed page from Karl Marx's *Value Price and Profit*, with attention to the words 'labouring power'. From the front cover of the Marx pamphlet the animation moves to the questioning face of the little boy.

> *…something equivalent to the arguments Marx puts forward in* Value Price and Profit *and so forth, which meant we had the idea of making a film which would in some ways, would've been quite abstract.*

Still: Bob Mathews shooting with his hand-wind Bolex camera.

> *Bob Mathews and Gerry Harant spent a lot of time going to meetings, explaining what we hoped to do.*

Archival footage depicts newly printed copies of *The Guardian*, folded and packed for distribution. Screen design introduces Bob Mathews in interview with moving image clips of *Prices and the People*.

BOB MATHEWS   (V/O)

> *I planned the script with Jim Crawford who was a journalist on* The Guardian *which was the Communist newspaper at the time.*

The screen design presents a collage in which a New Theatre actor from the 1946 New Theatre play *God Bless the Guv'nor* is matched with the same actor playing a young husband in *Prices and the People*.

BOB MATHEWS

> *We worked out an approach to the thing and an outline and finally Jim wrote the final script. And I - I shot it, I cast it from - any acting we wanted done, from the New Theatre people who were glad of the chance. And another New Theatre member we had do the commentary on it.*

Full screen *Prices and the People*. The original soundtrack and the newly voiced one momentarily coincide. We see people entering the Commonwealth Department of Trade and Customs, a comic performance of willing acquiescence from a 'public servant'. Two men exit from the building, congratulating one another and laughing together.

P & P NARRATOR (BRYAN BROWN)

Through this entrance go manufacturers and industrialists seeking higher prices - and generally getting them - no trouble at all.

We see trade union leaders entering the Commonwealth Court of Conciliation and Arbitration.

But when the workers asked the Arbitration Court for a wage rise the answer is nearly always…

The Judge solemnly, and repeatedly, shakes his head. Dissolve to a woman, a housewife with her purse, also shaking her head in a matching shot and a matching rhythm.

NARRATOR

The film sharply focused the creative and political differences between the filmmakers and the leadership of the Communist Party. This was a problem common to artists, writers and rank and file of the Party as it became increasingly doctrinarian and embattled as the Cold War proceeded.

Interview with Elizabeth Coldicutt:

ELIZABETH COLDICUTT

We made a great deal of the fact that cinema stands on its own feet as does music, as does sculpture, as does literature, as does drama, as does dance. They develop their own logic, inner logic and they survive by their own appeal. Not by any, put on afterwards ideological icing that might serve an immediate purpose but in fact falls away with the passage of time.

"…AND GENERALLY GETTING THEM — NO TROUBLE AT ALL."

A scene from *Prices and the People* showing a close-up of an artist's hand (Noel Counihan) drawing a series of cartoons illustrating *Prices and the People*'s argument about inflation and corporate profits at that time. The selection of shots from *Prices and the People* also metaphorically illustrate Ken Coldicutt's voice over.

KEN COLDICUTT   (V/O)

> *And we objected to the idea that the film had to be based on a particular campaign or that we should make a film which would have to be limited in its illustrations to the particular state of wages and prices which existed in that particular year, 1948. We wanted to make a film which would be much more general in its approach to wages and prices.*
>
> *In spite of all these objections, the Party leadership was convinced that they had to have this film and they agreed to pay the cost of production and for the six prints that they would use to send to every state in Australia.*

We see *Prices and the People* projected onto a screen. The scene shows firstly a trade union leader speaking to a crowd of workers and then smartly dressed women window shopping outside an antique shop.

> *The whole question is what use was made of the film? As far as our own activities in Melbourne and Victoria were concerned, very little use was made of the film. As for the five prints that we sent to other states, I have no indication at all any use was made of them.*
>
> *In general I would say it was simply a waste of our time and a waste of our money because it was our money. We didn't get a cent of what had been promised by the Party leadership.*

64

Prices and the People: CU, a hand grasps a bayonet. It is displayed hanging on a pawnshop wall; we see the pawnshop window. CU of a ticket on the bayonet 'curio – cheap'.

P & P NARRATOR (BRYAN BROWN)

Time payment business increases. Pawnshop advertisements come back into the trams. Effective price control is the people's only protection against this daylight robbery.

Elizabeth Coldicutt interview:

ELIZABETH COLDICUTT

I have no idea how it was when they were making the films but from May Day 1948 I can say clearly, we never ran a Party branch within Realist which would then have been answerable to the Central Committee. What we did was to grab people off the street who were interested in film and involve them in the work.

Screen design: graphic collage with torn and divided text 'Realist/Film, Communist/Party' and moving image from *Prices and the People* depicting, in close-up, the work of a butcher. A series of shots from *Prices and the People* follow, illustrating Ken's story.

KEN COLDICUTT   (V/O)

The support and assistance supposed to have been given to the Realist Film Unit by the party leadership was better described as sabotage. The cry was 'Oh our prices are too high'. And our prices in fact were half (of commercial prices). This left us in 1948 with a situation where we were in a tough spot. We had to drop those who were being paid, for example Gerry and Bob Mathews had to move out into more lucrative employment than working full time for Realist Film Unit.

Screen design: with Bob Mathews on the right of the frame and on the left the scene we have previously seen of the arbitration judge, slowing shaking his head.

BOB MATHEWS

Well I'm - I'd rather not talk about it, but there - it wasn't - it was really a - a one man show that - that film, as it turned out. My wife thinks it was my fault because Gerry was – (gesturing at the camera) turn it off and I can talk, you know.

INTERVIEWER O/S (DEANE WILLIAMS)

Sorry?

BOB MATHEWS

If you turn it off I could tell you, (pointing at the camera) but –

INTERVIEWER O/S

Oh okay.

Cut: the texture of TV 'snow'. A comic scene from *Prices and the People* illustrating the items used to calculate the CPI (Consumer Price Index), rises in the cost of living. A man with a table and chair made of packing cases, candles on the 'table', wearing pyjamas, is eating from a tin.

P & P NARRATOR (BRYAN BROWN)

Let's take a look at the average worker, living an average life. According to the basic wage price index. He's sitting on a box in an unfurnished room, eating tinned salmon by candlelight.

The comic scene continues as the man stands, displaying his patched pyjamas to the audience. Screen design collage: Ken Coldicutt still with the Certificate of Registration of a Business Name 'Realist Film Unit'.

KEN COLDICOTT   (V/O)

I was left as the sole full time worker, running the show. And although it was full time, I was not fully paid.

KEN COLDICOTT (V/O)

I reduced my basic wage to half and had to spend my nights and early mornings doing office cleaning to provide some support for my family.

From Ken's home movies we see a young boy pushing a pram past a fence where a white cockatoo engages them as they approach; Ken Coldicutt's first wife and children in a garden setting; Ken with the young family.

P & P NARRATOR (BRYAN BROWN)

Price rises are wage cuts. Keep price control, make it work for the people, not for the profiteers.

Prices and the People, closing scene. We see the various characters introduced in the film, the young newlywed, the elderly man, the waitress, casting their vote in the ballot box. We see crowds walking together while trains lie idle, we see a woman chalking a huge message on the road: 'Yes for Prices and Rent Control'

P & P NARRATOR (BRYAN BROWN)

Carry the referendum to control rents and prices. Throw your weight into the campaign to hold off depression by forcing wage rises from profits.

NARRATOR

The Chifley Labor Government's referendum was lost. Business and conservative opposition argued that this proposal for Commonwealth regulation over prices and rent was socialist interference with free trade and the wisdom of the market.

Screen design with images from the May Day march of 1946 moving across the background of a series of portraits of Ken Coldicutt, Bob Mathews and Elizabeth Coldicutt.

Despite the crisis over Prices and the People, *the Realists were no less committed to their beliefs. Their argument was with the hierarchy of the Communist Party not with the value of film culture and the necessity of social change.*

> "PRICE RISES ARE WAGE CUTS... MAKE IT WORK FOR THE PEOPLE, NOT FOR THE PROFITEERS."

The GREAT DELUSION

The autobiography of an
Ex-Communist Leader

CECIL SHARPLEY

Stanley Gilbert HAWES 14/1/22

about HAWES himself nothing to add to previous correspondence

CHAPTER 8
A POLITICS OF FEAR

Close up: Elizabeth Coldicutt

ELIZABETH COLDICUTT

My commitment to left-wing politics and any sort of activity is all very emotionally based, it's not really thought out. It's a reaction that's - I have to do something about it, just something practical, a little thing, but something genuine, something that might make a little difference here.

Archival black and white scene of a street march with Australian Communist Party banner prominently in the frame, and a superimposed image of a red flag, moving across the frame.

KEN COLDICUTT   (V/O)

The big membership that the Party claimed, about 20,000 at the end of the war, was largely a paper membership.

Screen design: Ken Coldicutt interview on the left of frame, and on the right a series of dissolves through a black and white title 'the Australian Communist Party presents', stock footage depicting Eastern European Communist state power, marches and demonstrations in Melbourne in the 1940s, concluding with an image of Stalin, and the frame divided by a kind of graphic war of words.

KEN COLDICUTT   (V/O)

Members had been gained partly by recognition of the correct policy the Party had pursued before the war in opposing fascism. It was gained partly by the prestige that resulted from the victories of the Red Army of the Soviet Union, the Red Army of China and the Yugoslav partisans under Tito.

The Party with that big membership failed to advance also because it did not make a correct estimate of economic and political conditions that existed in Australia and internationally after the war. And the Party did a great deal of damage to itself by continuing to support Stalinism.

Elizabeth Coldicutt interview.

ELIZABETH COLDICUTT

The time immediately after World War II until the McCarthy era is a time of energy and activity and organised activity and exchange of ideas and encouragement and belief that the public will accommodate what we're offering. But I suppose I do date the change in the atmosphere from the shock of the Sharpley nonsense. Hmmm. Such a person!

Cut: black and white Cinesound newsreel: 'Ex-Communist Disclosures: Sharpley Speaks!'

NEWSREEL COMMENTATOR

Former executive of the Victorian Communist Party, Cecil Sharpley, has aroused worldwide interest with a series of newspaper articles in which he made sensational allegations against communism in this country. He is interviewed by Reg Lennard, Chief of Staff of the Melbourne Herald.

REG LENNARD

What is your motive in exposing and condemning the people with whom you have worked for so many years?

CECIL SHARPLEY

I want to say emphatically and finally that my motive is to awaken this country to a very great danger.

REG LENNARD

And you say that danger is the Communist Party?

CECIL SHARPLEY

Quite definitely, and if you don't think that communism is a real menace in this country, you are living in a fool's paradise. The Communists are trying to destroy everything. They would destroy our democratic liberties even to selling out of this country.

"MY MOTIVE IS TO AWAKEN THIS COUNTRY TO A VERY GREAT DANGER."

CECIL SHARPLEY

Cecil Sharpley's defection from the Victorian State Committee of the Communist Party of Australia was announced with great fanfare by the *Melbourne Herald* who had negotiated exclusive rights to his story. The first articles appeared during the Easter holiday weekend of 1949. Sharpley's allegations were front-page news for weeks, months. They were compiled and sold as a pamphlet under the title "I was a Communist leader". A newsreel featuring the *Herald* Chief of Staff interviewing Sharpley was widely distributed through the major commercial cinema chains. Sharpley alleged that the Communist Party had been instrumental in rigging trade union elections, that it was financed from Moscow ('Moscow Gold'), that community based organisations of various kinds, like the New Theatre and the Realist Film Association, were no more than 'fronts' for the Communist Party and that it was dedicated to the violent overthrow of the state.

The Victorian State Government immediately announced a Royal Commission into Communism to be conducted by Justice Charles Lowe. The Royal Commission ran for almost twelve months and provided endless copy for the *Herald*. Other newspapers, such as the Melbourne *Age*, were a little more sceptical in their coverage. The Royal Commission's Report (May 1950) found most of Sharpley's specific allegations and claims could not be sustained. Royal Commissioner Charles Lowe found Sharpley an unreliable witness. He found that when union organisers were members of the Communist Party, and many were, their activities were directed in the first instance to the interests of their membership; simply put, they were conscientious trade union leaders. He found the Communist Party was not directed to the violent overthrow of the state.

The report was buried. During the period that the Royal Commission sat in Victoria the Menzies Government had come to power in Canberra. The preamble to Menzies' promised Communist Party Dissolution Bill simply claimed as fact all the allegations examined by the Lowe inquiry and found to be unsustainable. The day before Lowe's report was tabled in the Victorian Parliament, Menzies' Communist Party Dissolution Bill was introduced into Federal Parliament (April 27, 1950).

TRUTH ABOUT MURDOCH ROYAL COMMISSION

Sharpley-Herald Lies Are Self-Exposed

ROYAL COMMISSION INQUIRING INTO THE ORIGINS, AIMS, OBJECTS AND FUNDS OF THE COMMUNIST PARTY IN VICTORIA AND OTHER RELATED MATTERS.

The Victorian Government appointed Sir Charles Lowe to conduct a Royal Commission in April 1949 following allegations by Cecil Sharpley, ex-Communist Party state committee member. The Royal Commission ran for almost a year, spanning the period of a disastrous strike by Communist Party led coal miners and a Federal election in which the Chifley Labor Government fell and Menzies came to power. The findings of the Royal Commission were as favourable to the Party as could be expected under the conditions of 1949-1950. However a list of names (appendix D) compiled by the Commission of persons who were said to be or have been members of the Communist Party in Victoria was a source for ASIO for decades in identifying people for telephone taps and other forms of surveillance. The list included people who had never been CPA members, and did not mention others who were well known Communists. This list of names provided by Lowe's report constituted a list of persons who would be excluded from jobs in government, schools and universities, prevented from holding office in trade unions and potentially subject to arrest and internment if the Menzies Government so desired, had the Communist Party Dissolution Bill become law.

See: *MENACE*, John Hughes, 16mm, 96 minutes, 1976.

Vicky Rastrick, *The Victorian Royal Commission on Communism, 1949-50: a study of anti-communism in Australia*, unpublished MA thesis, ANU, 1973.

Cut: The swirl of spinning newspaper headline in the style of 1950s newsreel, newsreel 'Menzies Speaks', a sequence from *Menace* (1976).

MENZIES

The Communist pressure all round the world has been very, very cleverly designed.

The swirl of a newspaper headline spins into the frame a still photograph depicting the painted window display of the Melbourne Filmmakers' Cooperative cinema in Lygon Street, Carlton, July 1977. 'Last ditch resistance screening - all proceeds to the Co-op fighting fund: *Menace*.' A cartoon draws for its inspiration on a poster of the 1951 referendum campaign against the Communist Party Dissolution Bill, depicting Prime Minister Menzies on a 'wanted' poster, but here the profile of Malcolm Fraser (Prime Minister in 1977) has been added.

NARRATOR

In the mid 1970s I made a film Menace *about the Menzies Government's attempt to ban the Communist Party. At the time it seemed to me important to tell the story of the people who had struggled to defend democratic rights. This film from thirty years ago is now itself another oral history archive.*

Zooming in to a detail on the Filmmakers' Co-op window, the words 'now showing' fill the frame. Cut: film title: *Menace*. Archive footage shows Communist Party activist Ralph Gibson addressing a street meeting circa 1948, dissolve to Ralph Gibson in his lounge room interviewed for *Menace* (1976).

RALPH GIBSON

1949 was a very tough year generally. There were attacks on the unions, there were jailings, frame ups, violent disruption of meetings, bitter campaigns in the media. We had the lot.

You could say that democracy generally was under fire. Big business got worried about the

union gains in the previous years; the 40 hour week, gains in wages, in overtime rates, in annual leave and so on. And they were inflamed by the world situation too and the idea that they would soon be fighting Russia. Russia was presented at that time as just ready to swoop down on the world at the first opportunity. And so they attacked all along the line and in particular, they wanted to get the Chifley Labor Government out in the 1949 elections. They wanted to return a Menzies Government that would ban the Communist Party.

Spinning newspapers "I helped Reds to Rig Union Polls Sharpley tells how ballots are altered", "Red Secrets revealed by leader who left Party", "I was a Communist Leader" (*Melbourne Herald*, April 1949).

MENACE NARRATION (PAUL LYNEHAM)

In Victoria the Melbourne Herald *published a series of bizarre articles written by Cecil Sharpley. He claimed that the Australian Communist Party was controlled from Moscow and received 'Moscow gold' from the Soviet Union. The first article appeared on Easter Sunday. Two days later the Victorian Liberal Government announced plans to set up a Royal Commission on Communism.*

Screen design animation using graphic elements, the report of the Royal Commission, graphics from the campaign. Close-ups from the Royal Commission Report's Appendix.

NARRATOR

The Victorian Royal Commission continued throughout 1949 and into the following year. The Royal Commission reported Sharpley's claim that the Realist Film Unit was a 'fraternal', a Communist front organisation. The Royal Commission Report included an appendix with hundreds of names of those who were said to be members of the Communist Party in Victoria. Ken Coldicutt is among them.

Ralph Gibson

Home movie footage of Ken Coldicutt with his children, graphics from the Commission's report and Bob Mathews' home movie footage.

NARRATOR

Bob Mathews is also named. Another person on the list was Lloyd Edmonds. In Menace *he talked about the risks you faced if you were called a Communist.*

Lloyd Edmunds interview from *Menace* (1976).

LLOYD EDMONDS

They were a menace to society and not only were they a menace to society, they were a traitor. In fact it was thought that anybody who had political views and, mark you, you only had to be a little bit Left of what was a very, very moderate position to be regarded as a red in those days, I'm talking about during the Cold War years. Well that meant you should not and could not occupy any positions of responsibility. That is to say, you couldn't become a public servant – you couldn't become a public servant – anybody that was a bit Left was security checked.

Screen design animation with collage of documents and text 'secret'. Black and white ASIO surveillance footage follows people coming and going from a meeting at the New Theatre.

NARRATOR

For this purpose a new security intelligence organisation was established, ASIO, under the Chifley Labor Government in 1949.

Animated graphic with stills: Robert Menzies at the ballot box, and newspaper headlines 'Reds to be outlawed, banned from all posts'

The Labor Party lost the general election later that year and remained in opposition until the Whitlam Government, 23 years later. Menzies came to power in 1949, promising to ban the Communist Party.

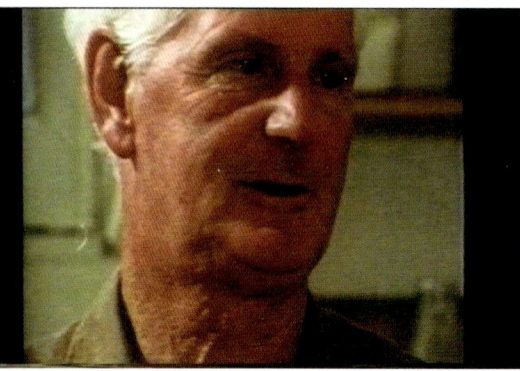

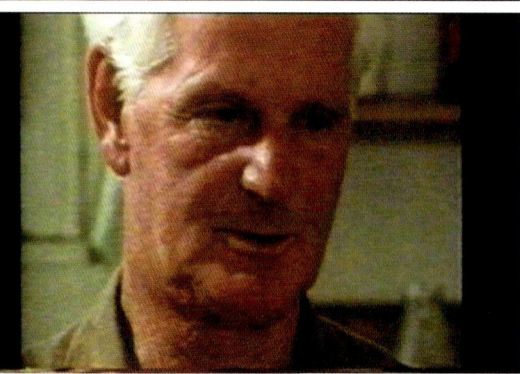

Lloyd Edmonds

Screen design with Ken Coldicutt on the left of frame, graphic collage on the right, "tighter security checks on all local reds".

KEN COLDICUTT   (V/O)

There was a great deal of intimidation during the Cold War period, especially after the Menzies Government came to power. Menzies greatly increased the strength of ASIO and used it to attack the left, to keep left-wing people out of the public service, for example like the - the National Film Board and its production unit.

Black and white video of Ken Coldicutt in the garden at his home, obscured by foliage. Graphic collage introducing the figure of Stanley Hawes, by citing Hawes' security file: 'Hawes, Stanley Gilbert', 'Film Division, Department of the Interior' collaged with stills from the *Realist Film Review* (1950).

"STANLEY HAWES WAS HIMSELF A SUSPECT."

STANLEY HAWES (1905 – 1991)

From 1946 until 1969, Stanley Hawes was the Producer-in-Chief, Australian National Film Board Film Division, later known as the Commonwealth Film Unit and later Film Australia. He was born in London. In 1931 he co-founded the Birmingham Film Society. He worked with John Grierson and the National Film Board of Canada. During his period with the Australian National Film Board, the Film Division of the Department of the Interior, the Commonwealth Film Unit and Film Australia he produced and directed over a dozen films advocating on behalf of government departments and the 'national interest'. During his career he was responsible for hundreds of films made by Film Australia and its predecessors. In 1970, he was awarded an MBE and the Raymond Longford Award from the Australian Film Institute. He chaired the National Film Theatre of Australia between 1970 and 1974, and in 1971 was appointed chair of the Film Board of Review. He played an important part in the 'renaissance' of an Australian film industry in the late 1960s. Stanley is on the record complaining about the interference in the work of the Commonwealth Film Unit by security forces. Unbeknown to him, ASIO considered him a security risk until a year before he retired.

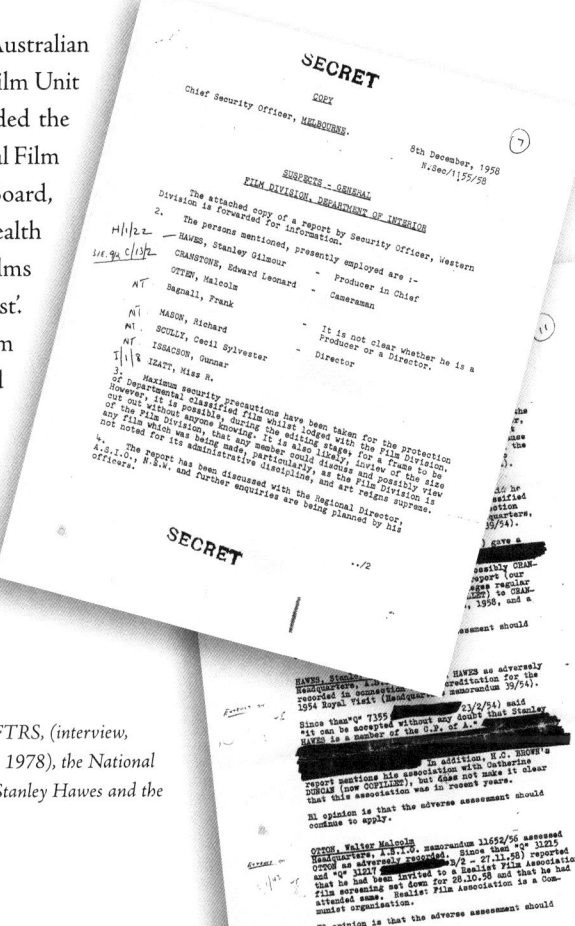

See: ABC Radio, Double Take, 1983 and records held by the National Archives of Australia, AFTRS, (interview, Graham Shirley, 1986), National Library of Australia, (interview, Joan Long and Andrew Pike, 1978), the National Film and Sound Archive, (interview, Albert Moran, 1991), Ina Bertrand 'Theory into practice, Stanley Hawes and the Commonwealth Film Unit' at on-line journal Screening the Past, July, 1999.

Stanley Hawes, Film Australia 1946-1970

KEN COLDICUTT (V/O)

When Stanley Hawes came to Australia from his work in establishing a Canadian National Film Board, when he was brought here to establish a similar organisation in Australia, he saw me and Bob Mathews and had a look at some of the work we'd done. He told me then that he would be quite happy to have me in his new film production unit.

And it was only some months later when I again met him in Melbourne that he told me that my name had been vetoed by security. And I found in the following years that the fact that my name was on ASIO's list, that I had an adverse assessment, prevented me from getting any other jobs.

Interview David McKnight, historian:

Animated graphic texts: 'espionage', 'subversion'.

DAVID McKNIGHT

ASIO was set up to fight espionage and subversion.

Espionage means people who act on behalf of another country, and who spy out the military and diplomatic secrets of Australia. Subversion is a much more cloudy concept. It involves essentially wrong thinking and wrong ideas. People who held wrong ideas were one of the targets of ASIO.

ASIO surveillance film.

Well the scale of operations by ASIO was vast. I mean they assembled what we call today a database, but it was in fact a filing system of tens of thousands, possibly over a hundred thousand files on individuals. So there was a vast apparatus of watching, observing and recording activities that were regarded as subversive. The apparatus of surveillance grew and grew and grew.

David McKnight, University of Technology, Sydney

"THE APPARATUS OF SURVEILLANCE GREW AND GREW AND GREW."

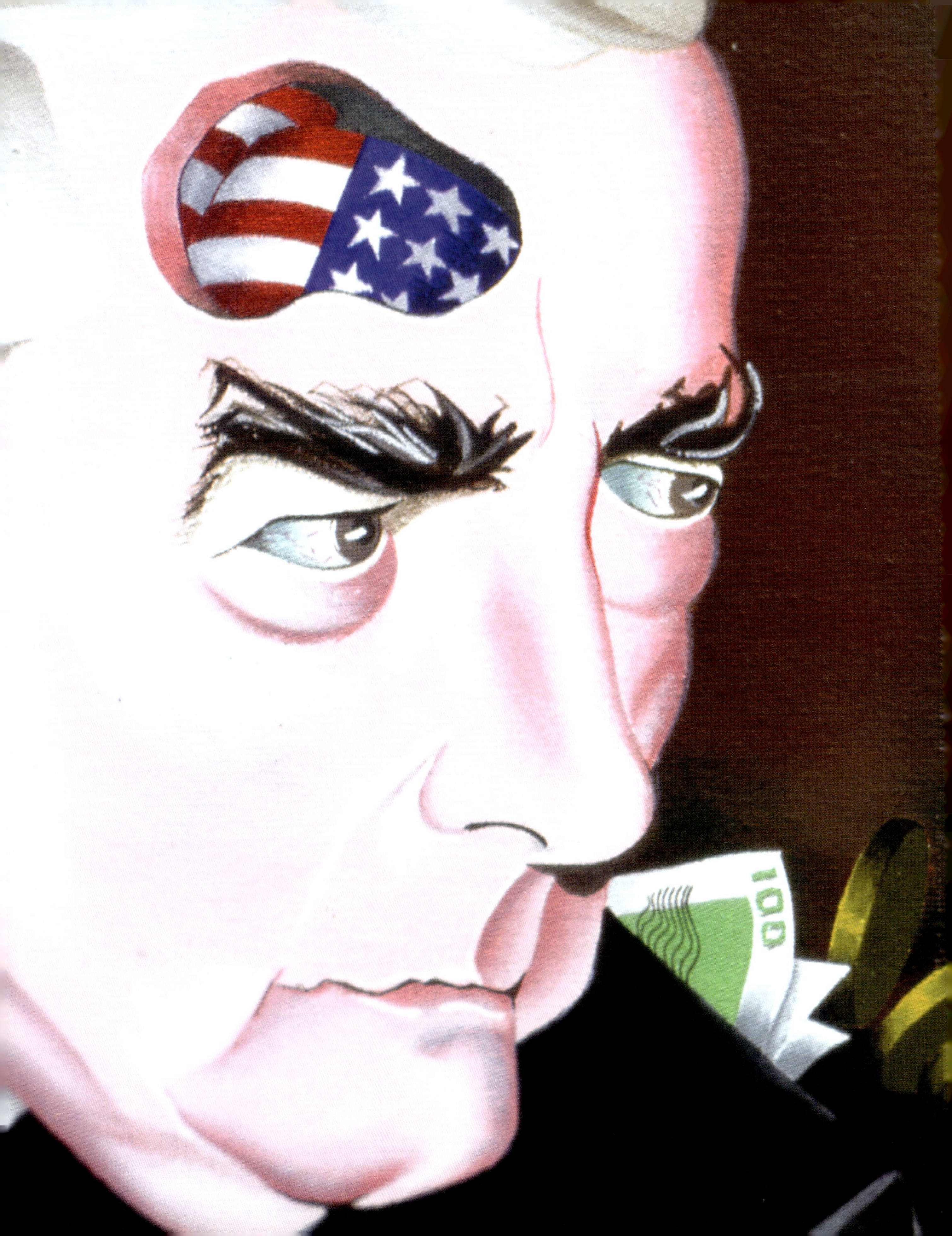
100

CHAPTER 9 PHONE TAPS AND NUMBER PLATES

ASIO surveillance film (continued).

DAVID McKNIGHT (V/O)

From the point of view of the ordinary members of the Communist Party, they were always totally bemused by the accusation that they were agents of a foreign power.

Rank and file members of the Communist Party saw themselves carrying on democratic and radical traditions of Australia.

And so the Left and the Communist Party thought that they were genuine radical patriotic Australians doing political activity, the best way they knew how. The others saw them as agents of a foreign power, but of course the Communists saw the Menzies Government and the security services as people who were betraying Australian interests because they were so deeply enmeshed with the British and the Americans.

Animated graphic collage: names and photographs of people named by Menzies in parliament as those who would be 'declared' and dismissed from their positions under his Communist Party Dissolution Bill, "Canberra Under Guard for Anti-Red Bill".

DAVID McKNIGHT (V/O)

I guess one of the things that this period shows is the way in which fear and suspicion can be mobilised, fear of the unknown, fear of the half known. This became a very potent political tool in the hands of the Menzies Government.

Animated collage newspaper headlines, stills of Prime Minister Robert Menzies.

MENACE NARRATOR

His Communist Party Dissolution Bill was introduced into Federal Parliament on April the 27th, 1950. The Bill empowered the

Governor-General on the advice of a special five-man committee to declare organisations and individuals as Communist. The names of people and organisations to be declared would be published in the Government Gazette *and it would be up to the declared person to establish that he or she was not a Communist within the meaning of the Act.*

Menace (1976), the 'dinner scene' in which Ralph Gibson outlines the scope of Communist Party Dissolution Bill.

RALPH GIBSON

A Communist was defined as anyone who supported Communist policies.

You know it was Communist policy, preservation of peace, it was Communist policy, socialisation of industry and so on. So that was a - a dragnet clause. Anybody who carried on after the ban, any work in which the Communist Party engaged or could have engaged, would be liable for five years.

Graphic animation: *Melbourne Sun* "Political and industrial Labor split on Red Bill", "NSW Labor says yes to Menzies: 'Push Ahead.'" Those mentioned in the narration to follow are illustrated with stills.

NARRATOR

The Communist Party Dissolution Bill passed through the House of Representatives with the support of the Labor Party, but it was held up in the Senate. Menzies declared a double dissolution and won power in both houses of parliament in the subsequent elections.

Following the death of Ben Chifley in 1951, Bert Evatt became leader of the Labor Party. When the Bill was passed the Communist Party and a number of trade unions challenged the Bill in the High Court.

THE COMMUNIST PARTY DISSOLUTION BILL

The Communist Party Dissolution Bill had a tumultuous passage through Australian Cold War politics. It was drafted with reference to similar legislation elsewhere, in particular in South Africa, where the equivalent Act – The Suppression of Communism Act, 1950 – was deployed in defending apartheid and enabled the jailing of Nelson Mandela and others.

In his Preamble to the Bill Prime Minister Menzies 'named' a number of people who he said would be removed from office when the Bill became law, as they were Communist trade union officials. This story made the headlines around the country. The government and the security forces were embarrassed when it was revealed that some of those named were not Communists, some of them were not trade union leaders and one was neither. ASIO's provision of these dossiers reflected the quality of the 'intelligence' that informed the governments authoritarianism.

A partially released file from the period ('CPA list of premises to be searched', NAA) contains only two of ten pages of addresses in Melbourne alone that were subject to the security services interest. These include private homes along with the Eureka Youth League and Communist Party meeting rooms and offices. Sydney Road Brunswick seems to have been a particular hotbed of dangerous subversives. Altona, Balwyn, Box Hill, Brunswick, Camberwell, Burnley, Caulfield, Reservoir, St Kilda, South Yarra, Williamstown are all included in the suburbs that could expect to be raided had the Communist Party Dissolution Bill become law. Scholars of the period are divided on the question of the likelihood of mass arrests and incarceration.

In November 1950 a challenge was brought before the High Court by the Communist Party and ten trade unions. The deputy leader of the Labor opposition, Bert Evatt, represented the Waterside Workers' Federation in their case against the Bill.

In March 1951 the High Court decided by six to one that the Act was in conflict with the Constitution and invalid. The Act was retrospective in its operations and provided the government opportunities to prosecute people without their having the right to defend themselves. One week after the High Court decision the Menzies Government called an election, dissolved parliament and, when returned to power six weeks later, drafted a Commonwealth referendum to change the Constitution in order to allow the Bill to become law.

The Labor Party was divided on the issue, but Bert Evatt's leadership, despite his own anti-communism, delivered Labor Party support for a 'no' vote. After an intense campaign, in which most newspaper and radio editorials and news coverage supported a 'yes' vote, the 'no' case won by a very narrow majority: 50.48% (September 22, 1951).

Michael Kirby of the High Court has written: "My grandfather would certainly have been 'declared'… the Court reached its decision against the clamour of public opinion at the time… I have come to appreciate the courage and wisdom, foresight and good judgement which the High Court of Australia displayed at that testing moment in the exposition of the requirements of Australian law" (Kirby, 1997). Commentators such as Justice Kirby, Julian Burnside and Jenny Hocking have noted the striking parallels, and concomitant dangers, of the Howard Government's 'anti-terror' legislation (2002-4) and the Communist Party Dissolution Bill (1951).

See: Leicester Webb, Communism and Democracy in Australia: a survey of the 1951 referendum, ANU, 1954. Peter Love & Paul Strangio, Arguing the Cold War, Red Rag, Carlton, 2001. Jenny Hocking, Terror Laws: ASIO, Counter-Terrorism and the threat to democracy, UNSW Press, Sydney, 2004.

Animated graphic illustrating the following narration with frames from Ambrose Dyson's cartoon booklet 'The Calamitous Career of Dictator Bob'.

NARRATOR

In March 1951 the High Court found the Bill unconstitutional so Menzies called for a referendum to change the Constitution to allow the Communist Party Dissolution Bill to become law.

Screen design graphic animation beginning with close-ups from Ambrose Dyson's cartoon for *The Guardian* 'Referendum Rd, Hitler's Hollow', the 'Vote No! 'Wanted' poster we saw earlier, modified for the window of the Melbourne Co-op cinema. Various 'Vote No!' leaflets.

NARRATOR

A poll six weeks before the September referendum reported an 80% Yes vote in favor of Menzies' proposals. Thousands of people felt personally threatened by the Bill. People buried books that could have been brought in evidence against them. Others made arrangements for relatives to look after their children should they be arrested.

Screen design animation sets a frame within the graphic collage on which we see spooling through in fast-forward a multiplicity of imagery from the 'outs' of the Realist films archive.

In support of the 'Vote No' campaign, Ken Coldicutt made a short silent film. In the trims and fragments of the Realist archives there is no trace of this 'Vote No' trailer. This is one of the lost Realist films. It was the last venture into filmmaking that Ken made.

Animated graphic collage showing *Realist Review* (March 1950) with its article 'Film Societies Come Together', and the ASIO documents cited in the following scene.

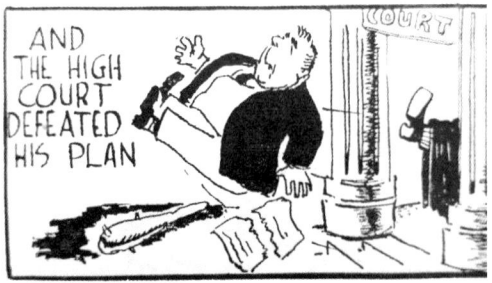

The Calamitous Career of Dictator Bob, cartoon booklet, Ambrose Dyson, Communist Pary of Australia, 1951.

NARRATOR

In March 1950 Ken wrote an article in a new periodical the Realists had established in which he reported on a national convention of film societies held in New South Wales the previous year. Ken had been working on establishing federations of film societies in each state and a national peak body the Australian Council of Film Societies. The New South Wales director of ASIO used this article as an attachment when he wrote to ASIO officers around the country.

VOICE OVER
(quoting documents)

'It is considered that the article is useful in that it sets up in some detail one of the methods by which Communists expect to penetrate the film industry.

They have already achieved some measure of success in this direction, but the extent of their success may vary to a considerable degree in the different states.

The attached article can be used as a basis for any investigation which may become necessary in this particular field.'

Super-imposed images, the projector continues, the documents specify film societies under surveillance in Victoria, ASIO surveillance footage.

NARRATOR

From this time on film societies were the subject of surveillance. Car number plates noted, agents sent in to secretly report on screenings and the people present.

VOICE OVER
(quoting documents)

"Coldicutt explained the meaning of films shown. From time to time his remarks took the form of subtle Communist propaganda. For example he discussed the influence of capitalism on the history of music during his explanation of one of the films."

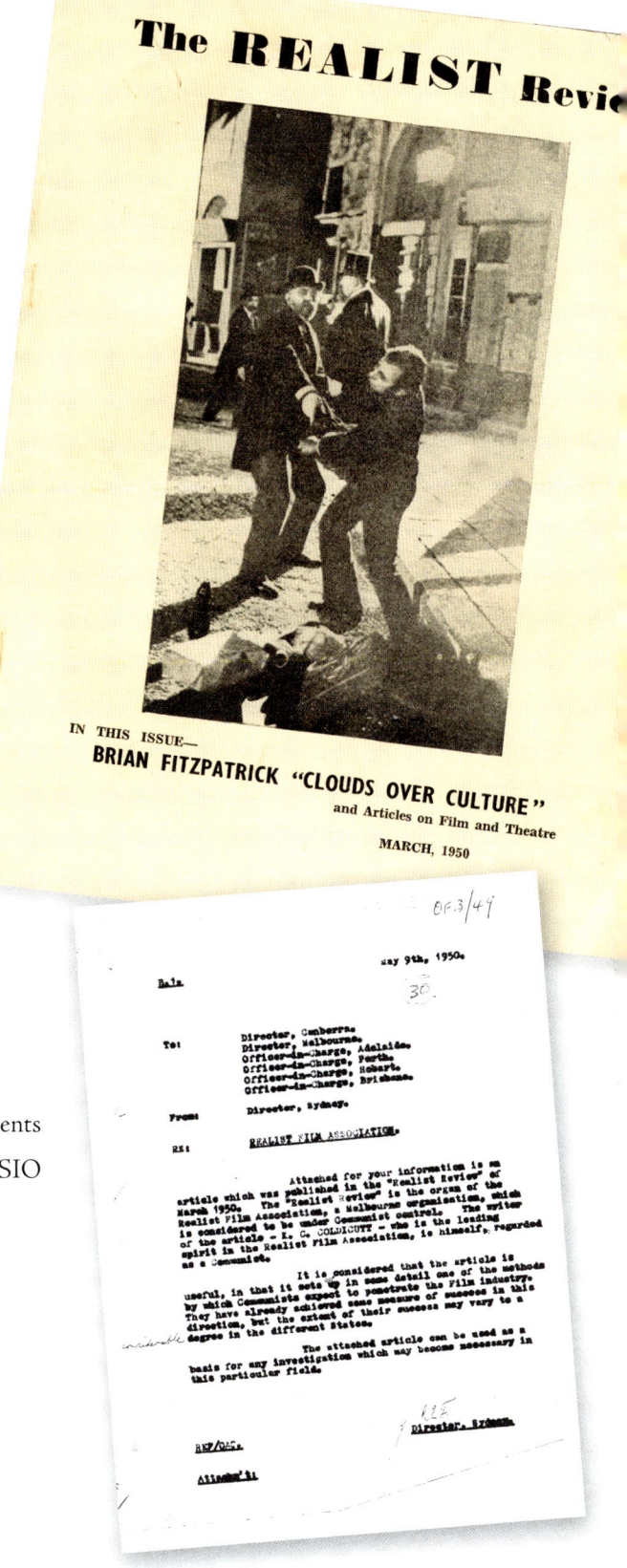

The New South Wales Director of ASIO used this article as an attachment when he wrote to ASIO officers around the country.

"Attached for your information is an article which was published in the *Realist Review* of March 1950. The *Realist Review* is the organ of the Realist Film Association, a Melbourne organisation, which is considered to be under Communist control. The writer of the article – K. C. Coldicutt – who is the leading spirit of the Realist Film Association, is himself, regarded as a Communist."

"It is considered that the article is useful in that it sets up in some detail one of the methods by which Communists expect to penetrate the film industry. They have already achieved some measure of success in this direction, but the extent of their success may vary to a considerable degree in the different states. The attached article can be used as a basis for any investigation which may become necessary in this particular field".

Director, ASIO, NSW, Sydney, May 1950

Film Societies Cor

By K. J. COLDICUTT

STIMULATED by the wartime circulation of documentary films, the film society movement in Australia began its belated growth in 1944. Since then, over thirty societies have sprung up in various parts of the country.

Increasingly obvious has become the need for a national organisation to co-ordinate the work of film societies, to facilitate exchange of information and supply of films, and to speak with one voice on such questions as censorship, tariffs, or attempts to stifle non-commercial screenings.

This organisation has at last been achieved as a result of a national convention of film societies held at the W.E.A. Hostel at Newport, near Sydney, on November 26-27.

The convention decided to form the Australian Council of Film Societies, to consist of delegates appointed by Film Society Federations in each State, or by individual societies in States where no federation as yet exists.

A constitution was drafted based on the constitutions of the N.S.W. and Victorian federations. A provisional committee consisting of Mr. Neil Edwards and Miss Betty Lacey of Melbourne and Mr. Vaughan East of Canberra was appointed to handle organisation until June next, when the Australian Council of Film Societies will be formally established by appointment of delegates from each State.

Immediate action was decided to demand increased grants for the National Film Library and its State agencies, such as the Documentary and Educational Films Council of N.S.W and the State Film Centre in Victoria.

Notable amongst those present at the convention were: John Heyer, of Shell Film Unit, recently returned from an investigation of documentary film production overseas; Stanley Hawes, Producer-in-Chief of the D. of I.'s Films Division; and John O'Hara, Chief Films Officer of the National Film Library, Canberra.

The only controversial issue during the convention was the British Code of Practice for Film Societies. It was suggested that adoption og the Code was a pre-requisite for Australian participation in the British Film Institute's scheme for an Empire Federation of film societies to circulate continental feature films.

Australian film societies have met with persistent refusal from most commercial distributors to supply feature films, and the British scheme, with its prospect of relieving the program drought, had strong attractions—strong enough in the eyes of some delegates to justify compromises with trade interests. Nevertheless, the Code was decisively rejected by the convention.

Most delegates saw clearly that the Code, which carried the approval of the British Cinematograph Renters' Society, would have the effect of keeping film societies small, exclusive and inoffensive to the trade. The Code requires that film societies should revise their constitutions to specify, for example, that no salaries shall be paid to office bearers, that membership shall be on a seasonal basis, and that admission to shows shall be by membership cards and guest tickets only.

The Code would prevent film societies from taking good films to broad sections of the public; it would discourage the screening of specialised programs which might have more appeal for outside groups than for members of the society. Excluded from the scheme would be a great proportion of the bodies now showing films non-commercially to audiences such as Parents' and Citizens' Associations, Church Societies, Community Centre Movements, and so on.

THE ARTS COUNCIL— AND WHAT IT DOES

1949 was a memorable year for the Arts Council in a number of ways. First, it made clearer the major post-war problems which face the Australian arts and the many talented young people who practise them. In this respect, the Council gained much valuable experience, for it sponsored nearly 100 different functions, giving opportunities to as many different singers, instrumentalists, dancers and writers.

Perhaps the most important step taken was the decision to reduce membership subscriptions from £1/1/- to 5/-.

Membership entitles you to concessions on all Arts Council functions at which a set charge is made for admission; not only will it bring you in closer contact with the arts—it will also lead directly to the encouragement of the arts and our young artists. Write to the Hon. Secretary, 3rd Floor, Collins House, 360 Collins Street, for further particulars—or ring MU3097.

Here is a list of Arts Council recitals during the next two months:
Wed., Feb. 22: Margaret Penington, clarinet; Ruth Hecht, piano.
Wed., Mar. 1: Margaret O'Callaghan, piano; William Allen, viola.
Wed., Mar. 8: Muriel Luyk, contralto; Sally Mays, piano.
Fri., Mar. 17: Peter Andrey, flute; David Fox, piano.
Fri., Mar. 24: Ronald Price, piano.
Wed., Mar. 29: Brendon Walsh, bass-baritone; Graham Hardie, piano.
Wed., Apr. 5: Sylvia Biddle, soprano; Eric Mitchell, piano.
Wed., Apr. 19: Ruth Price, piano.
Assembly Hall, 1.10-1.45 p.m.
Admission by silver coin.

Together

It was pointed out also that options are held by Australian distributors over many of the films promised in return for acceptance of the Code, so that it would still be necessary to negotiate with these interests before the films could be obtained. Having rejected outside dictation of the constitutions or forms of activity of film societies, the convention left it to the provisional executive to work out with the British Film Institute and Australian distributors an agreement suitable for Australian conditions, accepting necessary restrictions on screenings of commercial films, but not interfering with film society practices so far as other films are concerned.

AUSTRALIAN SURVEY

The Federation of N.S.W. Film Societies, first in the field, now incorporates Sydney Film Society, Independent Film Group, University Film Society, University Film Group, W.E.A. Film Groups in Sydney and Newcastle and film societies in East Sydney Technical College, Killara, Parramatta, Burrinjuck, Fairy Meadow and Wollongong, as well as groups such as Parents' and Citizens' Associations which include film shows among other activities. The Federation issues a duplicated bulletin entitled "Newsreel."

Sydney Film Society, oldest of New South Wales societies, usually runs two public screenings and a discussion group each month. It prints an eight-page monthly bulletin entitled "Film." Its audiences at central screenings have been as high as 600, screenings being thrown open to the public as well as to members. It has also arranged screenings and provided lecturers for other groups.

Independent Film Group, with a membership of about 300, runs two screenings a month, confined to members and guests. It prints a monthly folder containing brief program notes.

Sydney University Film Group recently organised a highly successful festival of silent film classics, with audiences as high as 700.

The Victorian Federation of Film Societies, formed in September last, has already taken action to secure revision of the Public Building Regulations to eliminate unnecessary restrictions on non-commercial screenings, where safety film is used. The Federation aims to serve the interests of Australian Film Society (Vic. Div.), Realist Film Association, University Film Society, C.S.I.R. Officers' Film Group, Religious Film Society, Y.M.C.A. Film Group, Kadimah Film Group, and film societies in Surrey Hills, Balwyn-Deepdene, Kew, Euroa and Olinda.

The Australian Film Society (Vic. Div.)—the inapt name is shortly to be changed to Melbourne Film Society—runs monthly screenings confined to members. Monthly discussion groups, recently tried, have not met with the success they deserved. The Society recently began the publication of "Film News," a monthly duplicated bulletin.

University Film Society has audiences up to 500. In 1949, its first film festival, held in the Union Theatre, met with such an encouraging response that a further festival is being planned for 1950.

In Tasmania, film societies exist in Hobart and Launceston. Exceptionally favourable conditions for growth arise from the fact that these societies have been able to organise public screenings of such films as OPEN CITY and LES ENFANTS DU PARADIS, which commercial exhibitors had considered too great a risk. The Hobart Society issues "Hobart Film News," a handsome duplicated monthly news sheet.

Film societies have recently been formed in Brisbane and Perth.

In Adelaide, the W.E.A. Film Club has functioned for some time. The recently-formed Adelaide New Theatre Film Society is meeting with a good response.

Canberra has had for some years a flourishing Film Centre, which publishes an occasional printed folder, "Film Progress."

FILM MEN MEET AT NEWPORT

The photograph shows three of the delegates to the convention of Australian film societies, which was held at Newport, New South Wales, during November, 1949.

Left to Right: Stanley Hawes (Producer-in-Chief, Department of Information Films Division), Neil Edwards (Chief Executive Officer, State Film Centre), and Ken Coldicutt (Secretary, Realist Film Association, Melbourne).

The Realist Review, March 1950

"...THERE WAS A VAST APPARATUS OF WATCHING, OBSERVING AND RECORDING ACTIVITIES THAT WERE REGARDED AS SUBVERSIVE. THE APPARATUS OF SURVEILLANCE GREW AND GREW AND GREW"
DAVID MCKNIGHT

REFERENDUM RD.
HITLER'S HOLLOW
NO!
AUSTRALIA
TUCKER BOX
McClintock

CHAPTER 10 VOTE NO!

Screen design animation draws on Realist newsletters, home movie footage and stills of Bob Mathews with his first family.

NARRATOR

> *The Realist Film Association continued screenings and expanding the work. Realist film societies were established in Adelaide, Sydney and Perth. But the conflicts between the Communist Party and the Realists continued.*
>
> *There was conflict and change on the personal front too. Ken Coldicutt and his first family had separated and early in 1949 Bob Mathews was divorced.*

From Bob Mathews colour home movies we see him launching a row boat, on holidays, with his new wife, Rivkah. Black and white archival footage from the Bob Mathews Collection, Warsaw, 1950, and scenes at Auschwitz.

> *In April 1950 Bob left for overseas with his new partner Rivka who was an activist with the Eureka Youth League. They were to travel to youth peace carnivals in Eastern Europe, to Berlin and Warsaw.*
>
> *Bob filmed these scenes at Auschwitz Concentration Camp in 1950.*

Bob Mathews' archival collection shot in Italy in 1950 depicting Carlo Lizzani shooting *Achtung Bandito!*

> *In Italy he worked as an attachment with the neo-realist director Carlo Lizzani and met with film distributors locating films for distribution in Australia.*

Black and white archival footage from Bob Mathews' *A Glimpse of New China*:

> *In 1951 Bob and Rivka joined a delegation to China where the Chinese Communist Party had come to power only two years before. This is when Bob shot the footage for* A Glimpse of New China. *ASIO followed all their movements with close attention.*

Rivkah and Bob Mathews

Bob Mathews, Carlo Lizzani, on set *Ashtung! Bendito*, 1950.

92

Screen design animation with a 'Vote Yes' poster from Brisbane: 'Oust the Reds and keep your freedom' – a 'Vote No' poster from the Building Workers Industrial Union depicting the 'masses' together closing the 'NO' gates against referendum fraud and the police state.

NARRATOR

While Bob and Rivka were overseas Menzies' referendum to ban the Communist Party had been the subject of intense and exhausting campaigns around the country. The September referendum results were very, very close. Western Australia, Queensland and Tasmania had a majority YES vote. While NSW, Victoria and South Australia voted NO.

The margin across the country was less than 53,000 people but enough to defeat the Menzies Bill.

We see George Seelaf in interview from Menace (1976):

GEORGE SEELAF

If the referendum had been won, well it wouldn't have been only the Communist Party that would've been affected. It would've been the left wing of the Labor Party and anybody who was progressive, anybody who was opposed to the establishment and wanted to do something in the interests of the working class; they would have been branded. It would have been a sad and sorry day for Australia.

Overlay newspaper cartoon from The Guardian depicting Menzies with his axe named 'referendum powers, for Communists only' about to chop at the tree called 'Australia Democracy' with its branches called 'free speech' etc. David McKnight is interviewed.

DAVID McKNIGHT   (V/O)

In a funny kind of way when the Communist Party Dissolution Bill was lost, the war on communism, the surveillance and the prescription of communists, continued. It was as if the Bill had been lost but it 'hadn't really been lost' and really

"IT WOULD HAVE BEEN A SAD AND SORRY DAY FOR AUSTRALIA."

we just kept fighting against the Communist Party in spite of the fact that the Australian people had said that they really didn't want to ban the Communist Party. It was a kind of de-facto ban.

A screen design collage showing the cheerfully happy couple Bob and Rivkah Mathews, and a text from their ASIO file pasted across their figures like a mug shot ID, then backdrops of the Sydney skyline, circa 1952, and pages for Bob's handwritten draft screenplay for the film *They Chose Peace*.

NARRATOR

When Bob and Rivkah returned to Australia they moved to Sydney. Bob had distribution rights and film prints from Europe and China. They dedicated themselves to the International Youth and Peace Movements and began planning another film.

Screen design animation with ASIO surveillance photograph of Vic Arnold taking part in the 'TV Make it Australian' campaign of the late 1950-60s, torn paragraphs from his ASIO file, and text derived from Realist Film Association roneoed newsletters announcing Ken Coldicutt's resignation.

NARRATOR

Meanwhile in Melbourne, Victor Arnold, another New Theatre actor and producer who had also been involved with workers' art movements in the 1930s became the new Secretary of the Realist Film Association, replacing Ken Coldicutt. Ken had become increasingly impatient with the Communist Party leadership's failure to comprehend the value of what the Realists were doing.

KEN COLDICUTT

After I resigned from the secretaryship of the Realist Film Association in August of 1951, I stayed on for a while as an honorary treasurer and in those few weeks I continued to send in accounts for the money owed by the Communist Party to the Realist Film Association.

Vic Arnold (left), 1958, Melbourne, Actor's Equity 'Make it Australian' Campaign (ASIO surveillance photograph).

VIC ARNOLD 1912–1982

Victor Arnold was born in London. He moved to Western Australia in 1939 and began his career as an actor with the Workers' Arts movement and the Labor Youth Theatre in Perth and Adelaide, where he was prosecuted for staging a performance of the anti war play *Till the day I die*.

The security services were reading his mail, breaking into his home and recording his movements from the early 1940s. He moved to Sydney and became a key figure in the New Theatre. Around 1948 he moved to Melbourne to work as an actor, director and administrator of the New Theatre and, in 1951, Secretary of the Realist Film Association, taking over from Ken Coldicutt.

He was named in the 1949 Royal Commission on Communism as a member of the CPA in Victoria. In 1958 he began his career as an official in the trade union movement as Secretary of Actors' Equity (Victorian Branch). He was a key figure in campaigns for Australian content on Australian television and fair conditions and pay for actors working in film and television. He died a little less than one month after retiring from his position as Secretary of Actors' Equity.

The records of Actors' Equity are held by the University of Melbourne Archives.

Animated screen design collage draws on Realist documents and stills showing Vic Arnold and Bob Mathews at the film poster exhibition, Olinda Film Festival, 1952.

KEN COLDICUTT

And until the time came, during one committee meeting, when Victor Arnold moved a motion that in view of the support and encouragement provided to the Realist Film Association by the Communist Party, he would move that - the debt be foregone. And I said that well the Communist Party had been responsible for nothing less than sabotage of a flourishing, and what could have been a highly successful organisation.

That produced a storm of course when the news got back to the State Committee and they sent me a letter asking to see me within seven days about this.

Black and white, slow motion moment of Ken Coldicutt derived from the Portapak half inch video interview, conducted by Graeme Cutts (audio from Wendy Lowenstein's interview, National Library of Australia).

I sent back a tiny note saying that I had heard enough bullshit from the Communist Party in my 15 years of membership to last me a whole lifetime and I'm not going to waste another minute of my time in having any discussions with the Communist Party leadership. And that was the end of any formal sort of acknowledgement by me of the Communist Party leadership.

NARRATOR

Around the time that Ken's resignation took effect the Russian film, The Fall of Berlin *was released in Australia.*

In a short excerpt from *The Fall of Berlin* (Mikhail Chiaureli, USSR, 1949), we see a cast of thousands, Mikhail Gelovani as Stalin, entering Berlin. Animated screen design introduces documents: - the minutes of the August 28, 1951, Realist Film Association debate on *The Fall of Berlin*.

"I HAD HEARD ENOUGH BULLSHIT FROM THE COMMUNIST PARTY IN MY 15 YEARS OF MEMBERSHIP TO LAST ME A WHOLE LIFETIME"

NARRATOR

It played over several nights to packed houses at the Carlton Cinema. The Fall of Berlin *with Mikhail Gelovani playing Stalin confirmed the Realist fears about what was happening in the Soviet Union.*

They recognised that the film's depiction of Stalin was symptomatic of Soviet totalitarianism. They convened a public debate on the film at the New Theatre in August 1951 roundly criticising it on aesthetic and political grounds.

GERRY HARANT

The Fall of Berlin *got all sorts of prizes in the Soviet Union and* Fall of Berlin *was fairly typical of all that was wrong with the Soviet film. It was all about Stalin evidently who fought the war on his own, he could have easily stood in for Errol Flynn and done a lot better. And he was shown in situations which were a lie because he was shown inspecting the troops in Germany. He never was in Germany.*

Document montage supporting the following commentary.

NARRATOR

Ken's critique of The Fall of Berlin *along with complaints about trade unions' lack of support for Realist activities, published in their Realist Film News contributed to his break with the Party.*

ELIZABETH COLDICUTT

Coldicutt went to Williamstown High School as a teacher, teaching chemistry. There must have been some sort of crisis that made Coldicutt walk away. There must have been just one last straw that broke the camel's back, but I don't remember what it was.

The Fall of Berlin (Mikhail Chiaureli, USSR, 1949)

We see colour and black and white home movie footage showing Ken and Elizabeth visiting a farm in the Victorian countryside with Ken's eldest son, circa 1952.

> "HE COULD HAVE THE JOB PROVIDED HE'D INFORM ASIO OF THE ACTIVITIES OF HIS COLLEAGUES."

> "I MADE IT QUITE CLEAR THAT I WOULD NEVER UNDER ANY CIRCUMSTANCES ACCEPT THE JOB WITH THE COMMONWEALTH ON THOSE CONDITIONS THAT I SHOULD ACT AS AN INFORMER."

NARRATOR

Ken and Elizabeth became partners, later settling on a small farm in Reservoir. Ken's home movies include footage he and Elizabeth shot in the mid 1950s.

They both continued their passionate commitment to working with film culture. For Realists, Ken ran 'Film Forums', screenings and lectures on film theory and world cinema.

Screen design collage with photographs and photograph album (from the collection of Ed Schefferle), with ASIO files on the Olinda Film Festival (1952).

NARRATOR

In 1952 Elizabeth, Ken and Gerry Harant were all closely involved in Australia's first international film festival held at Olinda outside Melbourne. This event drew crowds ten times greater than anticipated. This international film festival was the first Melbourne film festival. ASIO were there too of course.

DAVID McKNIGHT

One of the targets of ASIO was film festivals. Those festivals became places where ASIO wanted to know who was there? Who were running things? Who was importing these films? Because their job was to stop subversion.

ASIO surveillance photographs showing Ken Coldicutt at the second Melbourne Film Festival, held at Melbourne University, 1953. We also see documents from Ken's ASIO files related to his application for a job as Film Production Officer at the CSIRO.

NARRATOR

Ken remained under ASIO's surveillance. Ten years later when he was offered a job working in film with the Commonwealth Science and Industrial Research Organisation, the CSIRO, his security file continued to haunt him.

ELIZABETH COLDICOTT

After having been offered the job he was taken aside to an unfurnished room with two chairs and told that he could have the job provided he'd inform ASIO of the activities of his colleagues.

Screen design collage: interview Ken Coldicutt (black and white), with elements of his file superimposed.

KEN COLDICUTT

Even though I pointed out that it had been some years since I'd left the Communist Party and that I'd had no contact with the Communist Party since 1951, and that I had very strong ideological reasons for refusing to work with the Communist Party any longer, I still made the point that the Communist Party was a legal party and the Australian people in a referendum in 1951, had confirmed that it should remain a legal party and I saw no reason why I should tell anyone about the activities of the people who had simply been carrying on legal political work.

I made it quite clear that I would never under any circumstances accept the job with the Commonwealth on those conditions that I should act as an informer.

OLINDA FILM FESTIVAL

"A Landmark in Australian Film History…

The first Australia wide international film festival took place at a holiday resort in the Dandenong Mountains on January 25, 26, 27 and 28, 1952. Previous interstate gatherings had taken place at Newport NSW in 1949 and 1950, but no more than 60 people had attended. The Federation of Victorian Film Societies decided to organise a film festival on an ambitious scale, and booked accommodation for 80 people. The response to the news was staggering. When the Olinda Film Festival took place, almost 1000 people attended, including many who travelled to and from Melbourne each day and about 400 accommodated in Olinda for the weekend… The unprecedented success of the Olinda Film Festival is evidence of the growth of feeling against Hollywood domination of the cinema in Australia. Significant in this respect was the enthusiasm shown for the early Australian sound films and other Australian productions shown at the festival. There was outspoken resentment too of a system of censorship that is very kind to Hollywood but has made a number of attacks on films from other sources, culminating in the banning of *The White Haired Girl* and the hold up of *Daughters of China*, both films which were to be shown at the festival."

Extract, *Realist Film News*, April 1952

The National Film and Sound Archives has audio of radio interviews made for ABC Radio during the Olinda Film Festival.

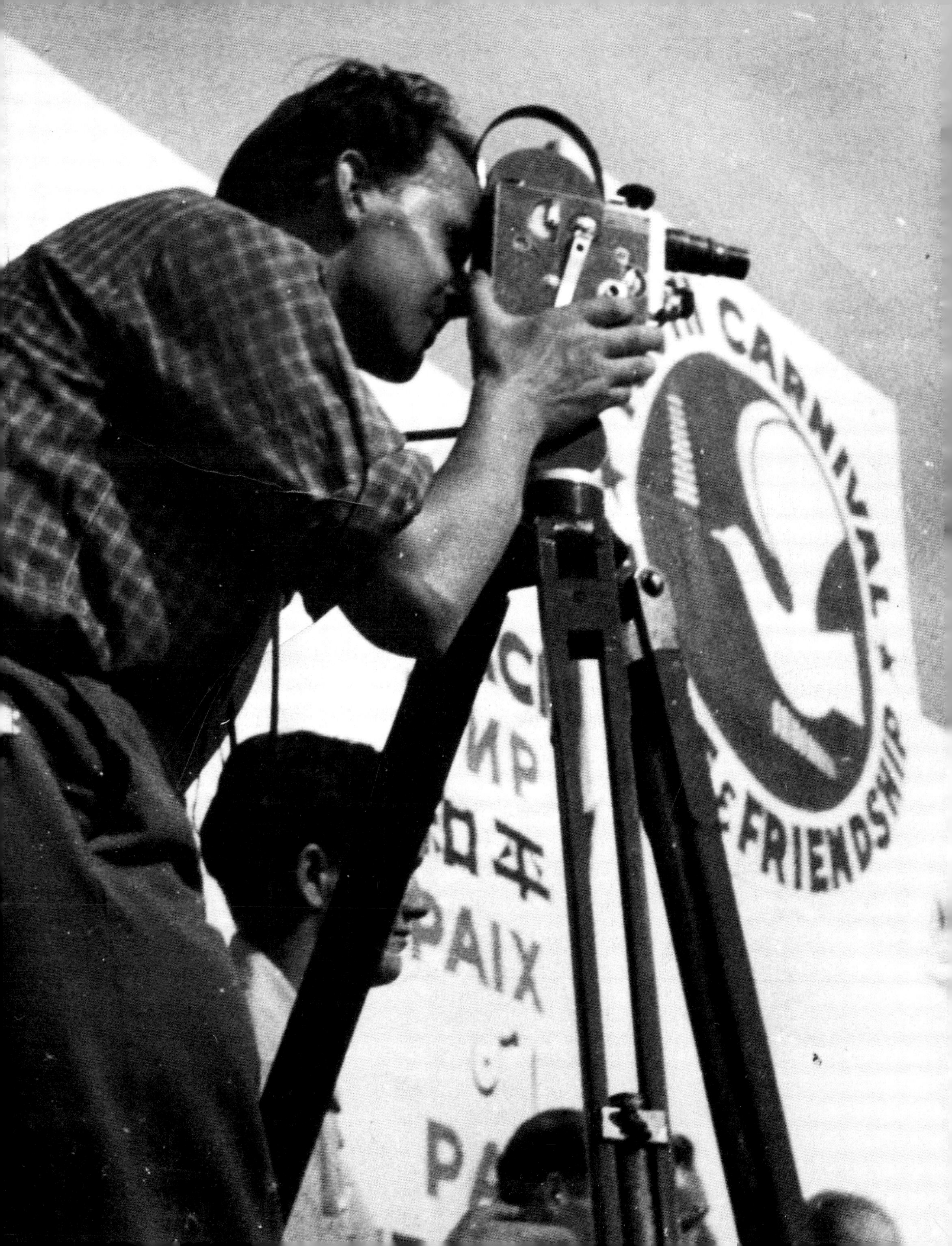
CARNIVAL
FRIENDSHIP
PAIX

CHAPTER 11 THEY CHOSE PEACE

International Youth Festivals were convened in Prague (1947), Budapest (1949) and Berlin (1951), and Peace Festivals in Paris/Prague (1949) and Sheffield/Warsaw (1950). The Sydney Carnival in March 1952 was one of the largest and most complex festivals ever to have taken place in Australia. A spectacular parade at Hollywood Park on the George's River near Bankstown followed by a concert and performance of Aboriginal dancers opened the festival's first day. There were cash prizes for sporting events staged at dozens of venues: three codes of football, cricket, tennis, table tennis, basketball, cycling, athletics, surfing, swimming, diving, wrestling, chess, billiards and snooker. There were art, science and photography exhibitions and awards (Arthur Boyd won a 'merit award' of twenty pounds). There were concerts, classical and jazz, literary and theatre events, a film festival and activities for children. It was huge.

ASIO, State and Commonwealth governments did their best to 'spoil' the event, but apart from success in denying visas to international guests, they failed. The extent of ASIO's 'Operation Handshake' during the festival has been attributed to the government's fear that the carnival could "morally cripple the governments rearmament programme", as Menzies had declared in March 1951 that Australia must be prepared for war "in not a day over three years". A notable feature of the carnival was the extent to which Indigenous participation was encouraged in every category of the carnival's activities.

See: Phillip Deery 'Community Carnival or Cold War Strategy' in Raymond Markey (ed) Labour and Community: historical essays, University of Woollongong, 2001. L. J. Louis, Menzies' Cold War: a reinterpretation, Red Rag, Melbourne, 2001.

Collage of still photographs, beginning with Bob and Rivkah, a domestic still, and then the ASIO surveillance photographs of Bob Mathews and dozens of others, greeting a New Zealand delegation to the Youth Carnival for Peace and Friendship, Sydney, March 1952.

NARRATOR

ASIO was also interested in Bob and Rivka Mathews. In 1952 Bob and Rivka threw themselves into work on an International Youth Carnival for Peace and Friendship in Sydney. This was to be the subject of the next film.

We see piles of files dedicated to ASIO surveillance of the Youth Carnival for Peace and Friendship held by the National Archives of Australia.

NARRATOR

The Treasurer of the NSW Peace Council was an ASIO agent and the files on the Carnival are extensive.

Colour archival footage of *Hiroshima* (circa 1948). An Australian naval officer strolls through the devastation of flattened Hiroshima. From Melbourne Realist archives we see anti-war graffiti of the Korean War period: 'Ban the A-Bomb'.

NARRATOR

The results of the American atom bombs dropped on Hiroshima and Nagasaki were alive in everyone's memory in 1952. Both Russia and America were conducting nuclear tests for ever more terrifying weapons.

Australians were fighting in Korea and the threat of another war, this time an atomic one, animated an international peace movement. This was itself another front in the cultural Cold War.

Collage: Bob Mathews shooting at the Youth Carnival, with pages from his handwritten screenplay, and receipts for film stock and processing.

NARRATOR

The film that Bob made on the Youth Carnival, *They Chose Peace*, was to be the last of their Realist Films.

Titles: 'Realist Films Presents', *They Chose Peace* 'Youth Carnival for Peace and Friendship Sydney 1952'.

NARRATOR

We have recreated the damaged soundtrack with new narration and effects. The text of the narration is as it was in the original.

THEY CHOSE PEACE
NARRATION (ORIGINAL)

If you had the choice - what would it be?

We see the opening scenes: footage from Bob and Rivka's China tour depicts enthusiastic Chinese men, women and children applauding and welcoming the Australian delegation to Peking (Beijing) in 1951. We see Rivkah, with her hand held by laughing children.

THEY CHOSE PEACE
NARRATION (DEBORAH MAILMAN)

If you had the choice, what would it be? To meet our neighbors in the Pacific with warmth and friendliness…

A montage of horrific war reportage, possibly the 'rape of Nanking'.

Or like this.

Continuing the opening sequence of *They Chose Peace*, we see stock footage, from the perspective inside an aeroplane, of bombs falling. We see bombs exploding in a South East Asian city, planes overhead, buildings burning, walls crashing down, people fleeing, children dying, crying and panicked by the bodies of their dead mothers.

Bob and Rivka returned full of enthusiasm for the growing peace movement, fearful of another war, this time the atomic conflagration that Prime Minister Menzies had declared may well be upon the people of Australia "within three years". They settled in Sydney. Bob directed the very successful *Reedy River* for the New Theatre and began work on a new film, a documentation of the planned Carnival of Peace and Friendship, Sydney, March 1952.

The Chair of the carnival's committee was blacklisted New Zealand filmmaker Cecil Holmes. The film of the carnival *They Chose Peace* was banned by the NSW and Commonwealth Government, and contested by a government-sponsored production *Menace* (Producer Jack S. Allan). The Carnival included a film festival, which was the precursor to the first Sydney Film Festival in 1953. Quality Films, established partly to provide films for the carnival, quickly became the principle, centralised Australia-wide non-theatrical distributor of primarily Eastern European films to the film society and educational markets. While the carnival's Chairman was Cecil Holmes, the treasurer of the NSW Peace Council was Dr. Michael Bialoguski, ASIO agent and later liaison for the famous defection of Vladimir and Evdokia Petrov (1953-54).

Deborah Mailman re-records narration for They Chose Peace

THEY CHOSE PEACE
NARRATION (DEBORAH MAILMAN)

Or like this?

Close-up: a tin of paste and a brush. Close-up: a poster is pasted to a wall: 'See you at the Youth Carnival for Peace and Friendship March 15-23 Sydney.'

Early in 1952 a number of young Australians made their choice, to oppose preparations for war with a carnival for peace and friendship. A carnival which would bring together youth from all corners of Australia and the world.

We see a meeting of young people around a table; a handsom young man (Sydney New Theatre actor, musician and peace activist Cecil Grivas) addresses those present. A young woman rises to present a report.

With the enthusiasm of youth they forged ahead. It was a colossal task, making great demands on their resources and small experience.

Committees and sub-committees grappled with the problems. Halls and playing fields had to be booked, accommodation arranged for thousands of interstate and overseas delegates. This was courageous planning.

ASIO surveillance photographs show Audrey Blake, 1952. Interview Audrey Blake.

AUDREY BLAKE

The idea for us having a Youth Carnival came from me. I said you know they are held all the time in socialist countries and we should try and break through and have one here in Australia.

I didn't realise it was going to be such a tremendous job.

From *They Chose Peace* we see boys in a schoolyard with pamphlets advertising sports activities planned as part of the carnival. We see artists working on a mural. We see the cast of Sydney's New Theatre rehearsing Oriel Gray's *Sky Without Birds*; the director, Jock Levy. We see workers on the docks with trophies.

104

THEY CHOSE PEACE
NARRATION (DEBORAH MAILMAN)

The idea of the carnival caught on. Interest began to stir among people all over Australia. Soon preparations for the carnival were in full swing.

Newspaper cutting. Low angle shots of plain clothes and uniformed police at a bus depot, montage of police at a variety of carnival locations.

The daily press reported the Menzies Government intends to wreck the carnival. Then began a systematic campaign to sabotage the carnival by every possible means. One example was the intimidation of those who had let their grounds and halls to the committee. All efforts were made to remove all evidence of the carnival; some councils employed a special squad. At all key carnival functions the impression was deliberately created by the ever present blue uniform that there was something sinister about this plan for peace.

AUDREY BLAKE (1916–2006)

Audrey and her husband of 66 years, Jack D. Blake (1908-2000), were prominent members the Communist Party of Australia. Audrey joined the Friends of the Soviet Union in 1931. In 1937-38 she worked in Moscow representing Australia in the Young Communists International. She was a founding member and Secretary of the Victorian branch of the Eureka Youth League, and a National Secretary of EYL (1941-52) and its successor, the League of Young Democrats. With the support of trade unions, the league contributed to an improvement in the wages and conditions of Australia's younger workforce, particularly apprentices and conducted workers' education in factories. The EYL was affiliated with the World Federation of Democratic Youth in 1945. Delegations of young workers and students from the EYL attended international youth and peace congresses throughout the 1950s and 1960s.

EYL member Graeme Bell and his Dixieland Jazz Band attended the first World Youth Festival in Prague in 1947. A year earlier the league convened the first Australian Jazz Convention. The EYL was very actively involved with peace movements here and overseas, campaigning vigorously against the Menzies Government's Communist Party Dissolution Bill and the conscription of young Australians for military training.

Audrey was part of the organising committee for the Youth Carnival for Peace and Friendship in Sydney in March 1952. Audrey and her husband Jack Blake were 'dissident intellectuals' within the Communist movement. Audrey withdrew from formal commitments to the CPA in the mid 1950s and finally resigned from the Party in 1966. Holdings related to her life and work are held by the La Trobe Library, State Library of Victoria, University of Melbourne Archives, National Archives of Australia and the National Library of Australia. Her personal papers are held by the State Library of NSW. She is interviewed in the documentary *Red Matildas* (1984) by Sharon Connolly and Trevor Graham. Her autobiography *A Proletarian Life* is published by Kibble Books, Melbourne, 1984.

Interview Audrey Blake.

AUDREY BLAKE

If the police and the Special Branch hadn't made such a fuss about it, I think it would've been a success, but a smaller one. And they always make that mistake; they made it big, because they - they - every single venue we got they took away.

One day a young wharfie came to see me and he was a tough young wharfie you know, and he got to the door, burst into tears! I was so surprised. And he - you know he came in and he said, 'Audrey they've taken every single place that we've got including our final place.'

Fairfield Park at that time was a big oval and a big arena. And so we had this tremendous struggle against us and that raised the whole question for us that we weren't going to be defeated.

A sequence from *They Chose Peace* at the Sydney Wharves with Margaret Walker and her dance group performing folk dancing, world music performances with workers and onlookers participating.

We see a man at a blackboard, striking out the black-listed venues.

THEY CHOSE PEACE
NARRATION (DEBORAH MAILMAN)

March the 11th, four days to the opening. The enemies of peace stepped up their attacks. More cancellations of halls and sports facilities, visas denied to overseas delegates.

From the International Film Festival, all Australian films withdrawn. All teams forced out of the surf carnival under threat of federal expulsion.

We see the New Zealand delegation arriving at the wharves and being welcomed by carnival hosts, and the surveillance photographs as a kind of 'reverse angle'.

Audrey Blake, Sydney, 2004.

AUDREY BLAKE   (V/O)

The Chinese were refused visas, they were going to send quite a big delegation. The only delegation was the New Zealanders. They were really dancing and carrying on, wonderful. There was a tremendous feeling of resistance growing up among the people, to be so blatantly interfered with. The place was smothered in police.

NARRATOR

ASIO photographed and indexed everyone who turned up to welcome the New Zealand delegates, while Bob Mathews and others shot their scenes for They Chose Peace.

Screen design collage with the leaflet produced to encourage supporters to protest against the banning of They Chose Peace.

When the film was finished it was banned by the New South Wales censor who demanded cuts before the film could be exhibited. Among the footage under Sue Mathews' house we found one of the deleted scenes. Three shots and one paragraph of narration.

A wide shot of a large street recruitment poster 'Australia Needs You', 'Serve to save Australia Join the Army, Navy, Air Force', Three smiling faces of the services: 'This is the Life'.

THEY CHOSE PEACE
NARRATION (ORIGINAL)

But there are men with other plans for you. Men who intend that the youth of the world should meet on the battlefield. For these it became urgent that the carnival should be destroyed.

The daily press reported the Menzies Government intends to wreck the carnival…

Dissolve through film rolling through the gate of a projector, to a new presentation title: 'The National Films Council of the Motion Picture Industry of Australian presents *Menace*' (1952), against the background of an exploding atomic bomb.

YOUTH CARNIVAL FOR PEACE AND FRIENDSHIP

"In spite of bellicose threats of the authorities who declared that the carnival would never take place, and in spite of the vindictive attempts to put every possible obstacle in the way of the organisers, the carnival not only took place but proved a single success. While we cannot chronicle the carnival as a whole, we record that during the International Film Festival organised as part of the carnival, the following films were given their Australian premiere: the Chinese films *The White Haired Girl* (as cut by the censor) and *Daughters of China*; the Soviet prize winner *Cavalier of the Gold Star*; and the Polish films *The Last Stage* and *That Others May Live* (also known as *Border Street*). Realist Film Association's colour production *Australians in Berlin* played a part in the campaign before the carnival, and Realist cameramen helped in shooting the carnival itself."

Extract, *Realist Film News*, April, 1952

Arrange Private Screenings

- Insist on your right to see this film and judge for yourself.

- Organise your own private screenings of the film they do not want you to see.

- Projectors and operators available to screen the film anywhere and everywhere.

☆

For further particulars apply—

REALIST FILM ASSOCIATION
92 FLINDERS STREET, MELBOURNE.   C. 4845.

Coronation Press Pty. Ltd.

BANNED
FILM MUST BE RELEASED

"THEY CHOSE PEACE"—the factual film story of the Australian Youth Carnival for Peace and Friendship held recently in Sydney, has been banned in N.S.W. by Mr. Kelly, Chief Secretary.

The Commonwealth Censor who carries out the policy of the Commonwealth Government, also proposes certain cuts and alterations before he will pass the film for public screenings in Victoria.

CENSORED

1. All references and critical comments on the warlike policy of the Menzies Government (which, as recent by-elections reveal, has lost the people's confidence).

2. Exposure of methods used to disrupt the Youth Carnival for Peace and Friendship.

3. The criminal neglect by the Government of the Aboriginals. (The Chief Censor says the natives of Australia are well treated and have opportunities, but are lazy.)

4. A banner in a scene in the film saying: "Build Homes, Schools and Hospitals."

These outrageous demands aimed at stifling criticism of certain Government actions are a negation of our democratic and civil liberties.

We call upon all peace loving and democratic Australians to resist this dangerous attack on freedom of expression and comment.

DEMAND

- That the ban on the film "They Chose Peace" be lifted!

- An immediate end to all political censorship and thought control!

- The right to freedom of expression and to advocate peace!

PROTEST

- The Commonwealth Censor, Bligh Street, Sydney, N.S.W.

- The Chief Secretary, Parliament House, Sydney, N.S.W.

- The Minister for Trade and Customs, Canberra, A.C.T.

NARRATOR

During that same year the government's film production agency made their own film, Menace, *which was widely distributed by the British and American cinema chains.*

Menace *was written with the approval of the head of ASIO, Charles Spry, and edited at Twentieth Century Fox with donated footage from the commercial newsreels.*

From *Menace* (1952) we see newsreel footage of Stalin moving up a stone staircase to oversee a military parade. A globe of the world turns, the opening ceremony of the Carnival for Peace and Friendship.

MENACE (1952)
NARRATION (HARRY DEARTH)

The same emblems of tyranny are to be seen in Australia today. Little knowing what they do, our youth are learning to pipe to the tune called by Moscow.

Their Communist banners and slogans talk of peace and friendship. Peace and friendship with whom? The Communists?

Menace (1952) continues, Australian soldiers marching through the streets of Sydney on their way to Korea.

The very people that these men are going to fight so that democracy can survive?

From ASIO surveillance photograph, Bob Mathews with his hand-wind Bolex shooting the carnival scenes at the wharves. From *They Chose Peace* - the 'Colliers scene.

THEY CHOSE PEACE
NARRATION (DEBORAH MAILMAN)

In the midst of the celebrations the magazine AM *sounded a dangerous note by publishing this war propaganda.*

We see Deborah Mailman recording the re-voiced narration at the studios of Music and Effects in Melbourne.

MENACE

Menace (1952) was made by the government's film production house, at that time the Film Division of the Department of the Interior - later Film Australia. The unit was established in 1941 within the newly formed Department of Information established to manage government public relations in the early days of WW2. In the early post-war period the government's film division was re-invented under the direction of an Australian National Film Board, established in 1945. The Producer-in-Chief was Stanley Hawes.

However, the unit that produced *Menace*, Australian Diary Unit operated virtually autonomously, reporting to the Department of Information and, after 1949, to the Department of the Interior, rather than to the Producer-in-Chief of the Film Division. Australian Diary made over 130 magazine entertainment newsreels through to 1970. These were widely distributed through an agency established during the war to manage wartime propaganda in the cinemas: the National Films Council of the Motion Picture Industry of Australia (Hoyts, Greater Union, Metro-Goldwyn-Mayer), Secretary: Jack S. Allan.

Menace and *One Man's War* (Tom Gurr, 1952), advocating Australia's involvement in the Korean War, are examples of Cold War propaganda newsreels made by Australian Diary. *Menace* was made at the suggestion of Ernest Turnbull, head of Hoyts Cinemas, and with the support and approval of Wilfred Kent-Hughes, Attorney General, and Charles Spry, Head of ASIO. Jack Allan wrote to Charles Spry, describing the film as "a pretty scorching indictment of the menace of communism". He invited ASIO to vet the script, which they did in June 1952. The conclusion of the film is an assault on the Youth Carnival for Peace and Friendship. *Menace* was provided the most widespread exhibition of any government produced film; released in September 1952 through Hoyts, Greater Union and MGM cinemas. Jack retired in 1964.

Like other Australian Diary projects it was cut at Twentieth Century Fox in Sydney (the owner of Hoyts), with 13,000 feet of international communism footage donated by Twentieth Century Fox, Hollywood.

JACK S. ALLAN 1899-1968

A senior producer for the Australian National Film Board (later to become Film Australia), Jack Allan was given control of the Australian Diary Unit in 1947. He was responsible for about 130 Australian Diary newsreel magazine films that were produced from the Commonwealth Department of Information's head office in Sydney and edited at Twentieth Century Fox's Movietone studios. They were widely distributed in commercial cinemas through to the early 1960s. His credits as director include *Sun Gods of the Surf* (1945), *Surf Patrol* (1950), *The Farmer was a Fighting Man* (1953), *Saga of a City* (1957), *Talkabout Australian Territories* (1963) and *Place for a Village* (1966). As producer *Jungle Patrol* (1945), *One Man's War* (1951), *Menace* (1952), *Training Champions* (1957) and *You and Your Vote* (1963) are the more notable productions.

Dick Mason refers to Jack S. Allan's involvement in the blacklisting of Cecil Holmes at the Commonwealth Film Unit in the mid 1960s. See interviews: Richard (Dick) Mason.

An American artist's impression of the destruction of Moscow by an atom bomb.

From *They Chose Peace*, peace activists march to Consolidated Press in Sydney, and occupy the buildings foyer.

THEY CHOSE PEACE
NARRATION (DEBORAH MAILMAN)

> *Wishing for peace is not enough. Peace must be fought for. So from the Carnival came a delegation to join with the Australian Peace Council in a protest against the publication of war propaganda.*

Young people lay wreaths at the war memorial in Taylor's Square, Sydney, 'A tribute to all Australians who died for a lasting peace, from the Australian Peace Council'.

> *These young people consider that such activity against war is a debt we owe to the ordinary Australians who gave their lives so that we might live in peace.*

Audrey Blake interview.

AUDREY BLAKE

> *The whole question of how people become political, quite often it's the other side of politics who make the running, because they try and stop what is; then - it was - they would say 'everything was Communist'.*

> *Everything wasn't Communist. But it's true that wherever there were a few Communists, there's no doubt about it, they did work and they did organise and they did try and always work with other people. And our mistakes were very big because you know our support for the Soviet Union was unthinking - no it wasn't unthinking - it was wrong thinking.*

> *We did not understand the question of Stalinism and I just hope that people are able to see what was some of the positive things that we did know and we did do.*

Carnival souvenir shoehorn and ribbon.

Opening parade, Youth Carnival for Peace and Friendship, Sydney, 1952.

Closing march, Youth Carnival for Peace and Friendship, Sydney, 1952.

From *They Chose Peace* we see sequences from the Aboriginal settlement at La Perouse, and Faith Bandler as a young woman, speaking to the assembled crowd, a mixture of Indigenous and non-Indigenous people, enjoying a performance of folk music and dance.

THEY CHOSE PEACE
NARRATION (DEBORAH MAILMAN)

For the Indigenous people of Australia there has never been a time of real peace. Isolated from the rest of the community into drab settlements, refused the rights of citizenship and the right to live decently, they realised only too well the importance of the message the carnival brought them.

And the friendship and mutual respect which grew up between them and carnival delegates became a token of the time when the Aboriginal people would stand in their full stature.

The closing sequences from *They Chose Peace* show a huge street parade. Men and women applaud from the steps and pavements, speakers address the crowd, the carnival flag waves triumphantly, with its special emblem, the dove of peace and the boomerang.

On the last day came a triumphant march through the streets of Sydney. So strong had support grown around the carnival that police granted permission for the most spectacular peace parade ever staged in Australia.

This was the carnival the Menzies Government intended to wreck. One of the greatest crowds ever seen in the Sydney Domain had turned out to celebrate the climax. Those who profit from war had been defeated. The carnival with its great theme of peace and friendship had won the day.

Here were the youth who made their choice, peace not war, friendship, not racial hatred. They had proved their strength, proved that they can and will win the fight for mankind's highest cause, the cause for peace and friendship throughout the world.

Jan Blake leads the opening parade, Sydney, 1952.

York Times.

The New York Times Company

TUESDAY, JUNE 5, 1956.

Partly cloudy today; fair tonight and tomorrow.
Temperature range today: 73-60
Temperature range yesterday: 73.2-58.6

FIVE CENTS

KHRUSHCHEV TALK ON STALIN BARES DETAILS OF RULE BASED ON TERROR CHARGES PLOT FOR KREMLIN PURGE

OWS AND PLAN

British Effort ection

olutions ge 5.

LTON

N. Y. Council today a g Ham- his good npliance rmistice and So- reed at to elim- g for a ne ques- ceptable

nch del- morning watering olution. d twice o meet e para- direct at ab- nthony ster, thony's cted to tention nt must e with of 1947.

Britain he vote minate ph had amper- of the

A GOOD TIME IS HAD BY ALL: Yugoslavia's President, Marshal Tito, right, and Soviet Premier Nikolai A. Bulganin, left, enjoying a light moment with their aides at the Premier's offices in the Kremlin. In addition to Premier Bulganin on Soviet side of table are, from left, Dmitri T. Shepilov, Foreign Minister, and Nikolai P. Firyubin, Ambassador to Yugoslavia. Next to Marshal Tito is his Vice President, Dr. Edvard Kardelj.

TITO LINKS AMITY TO SOVIET REFORM

Tells Russians Future Ties Depend on Shift From Line

Capital Can See No Change In the Soviet System Itself

By DANA ADAMS SCHMIDT
Special to The New York Times

WASHINGTON, June 4—Diplomats and other officials construe Nikita S. Khrushchev's speech to the Twentieth

U. S. ISSUES A TEX

Dead Dictator Paint as Savage, Half-Ma and Power-Crazed

Khrushchev talk, as release by Washington, Pages 13-16

By HARRISON E. SALISBU
Special to The New York Times

WASHINGTON, June 4—T text of Nikita S. Khrushche secret speech attacking Stal as published by the State partment today, describes t late dictator as a savage, ha mad, power-crazed despot.

The speech shows that t old dictator utilized the Sov and Communist apparatus to e tablish a rule based on terr torture and brute force.

Stalin, as he is pictured Mr. Khrushchev, turned t world about him into a miasm of treachery, treason and nigh marish plots. The picture w one that beggared the wilde surmise of political opponents communism.

At the time of Stalin's dea he was embarked upon a pl that, in Mr. Khrushchev's op ion, had as its objective the "wiping out" of all the old members of the top Kreml leadership.

Mr. Khrushchev said Stal

CHAPTER 12 **1956 AND AFTER**

Dissolve through from the emblem of the Youth Carnival flag to a slow zoom in to Bob Mathews' profile from the still with which the *They Chose Peace* sequence began, Mathews filming with his Bolex against a background of the carnival's emblem. Dissolve through the closing card from *They Chose Peace* 'End' (black and white) against the logo.

NARRATOR

While we were editing the sequence about Bob's last film They Chose Peace, *his daughter Sue called up to say that Bob had just passed away.*

Dissolve to an exterior, Monsalvat in the Melbourne suburb of Eltham, where in a series of stills we see the setting and guests at a memorial service for Bob Mathews. Sue Mathews is speaking to assembled mourners.

NARRATOR

During her eulogy at his funeral Sue spoke about how Bob was among the thousands of people who'd turned away from the Communist Party after the horror of the Stalinist regime was denounced by the new Soviet leader, Nikita Khrushchev.

Slow zoom in to a still photograph of Bob Mathews, dissolve through to a moment from his home movie footage – a shot we have seen before – showing the shadows of Rivkah and Bob ahead of them as they walk along a bush track. We see the shadow figure of Rivkah waving, followed by a shot of Bob walking toward camera, Rivkah and Bob playing on a winter beach.

SUE MATHEWS

In 1956 everything changed. At the 20th Congress of the Communist Party of the Soviet Union, Nikita Khrushchev revealed the truth about the Stalinist era and its labour camps.

In town that evening Bob heard the paperboys call, bought a paper and, despite the cold, the wind and falling darkness, spent an hour propped

RFA NATIONAL CONFERENCE, 1955

"The first national conference of Realist film groups in Australia was held during the first weekend in September, convened by the Realist Film Association of New South Wales. A total of eighteen delegates represented 10 groups in New South Wales, Queensland and Victoria. 14 visitors attended, representing several organisations, including trade unions. We sent two delegates. Groups in Western Australia, South Australia and Tasmania sent written reports… Among the decision of the conference was the establishment of a liaison committee in Sydney to deal with current problems about the importation and exhibition of films…"

Extract, Realist Film News *October – November 1955.*

up against the wall of the Melbourne Town Hall, reading, shocked and stunned as the faith drained out of him. Bob left the Party and never forgave socialism.

From Bob Mathews home movie footage (continued) Bob throws a picnic rug over the camera. From the blanket's red texture we dissolve through to animated screen design with Mikhail Gelovani as Stalin, Nikita Khrushchev and the documents supporting the following narration – the minutes of the 1951 *Fall of Berlin* meeting, the invitation to the 'aggregate meeting of cultural faction', Ken's typed notes of his presentation.

NARRATOR

Ironically Khrushchev's de-Stalinisation speech used the film The Fall of Berlin *to illustrate what Khrushchev called the 'cult of personality' that had been built up around the figure of Stalin. The Arts Committee of the Communist Party of Victoria held a meeting in Melbourne to discuss Khrushchev's speech and Ken Coldicutt was given permission to speak.*

He pointed out that the Realists had sought five years earlier to open up debate about Stalinism around the film The Fall of Berlin, *but had been ignored.*

Close up: 'K.J.C.'s remarks to Arts Aggregate…' a montage of key words and phrases from Ken's statement: 'art workers', 'concrete sensuous images', 'second-class citizen'. Dissolve through to the wide shot tableau from *A Place to Live* of a family living in a shanty, a young mother handing a cup to an elderly man in a wheelchair and a boy leaving for school, kissing his mother goodbye.

NARRATOR

He said that the party needed to recognise that "the artist is not a second-class citizen". He said, "ideas expressed by the artist in concrete sensuous images are just as important as those expressed by the political leader in the abstract phrases of a political document".

Ken Coldicutt's address to the CPA Arts Committee, 1956 (page one)

Dissolve to the foyer of ACMI (Australian Centre of the Moving Image) in Melbourne where an elderly man with crutches is entering a cinema. We see a number of people enter the cinema, among them Sue Mathews. Cut to the cinema interior, where *A Place to Live* is screening. The voice of John Flaus is reading from newspaper reports of 1947 screenings of *A Place to Live*, Melbourne, 1947. We see full screen a series of images from the film, seen earlier.

JOHN FLAUS (V/O)

Melbourne Sun News Pictorial, *Friday 20th June, 1947*, page one: "In shocked silence 500 people watched the slum film at the Assembly Hall last night. The film, a stark expose of the slums in Fitzroy, shows children in bug-ridden cots, families in rat infested rooms, houses without baths or wash troughs, and back streets littered with dead cats and heaps of tin. Father Tucker, Superior of the Brotherhood who gave a commentary on the film, said he wanted the film shown throughout Victoria to awaken people to the horrors of the slums."

Interior ACMI cinema, Melbourne. Elizabeth Coldicutt approaches the microphone.

ELIZABETH COLDICUTT

What drew me to Ken Coldicutt was his unswerving lifelong political commitment, his wish to change the world - more modestly, to change the world around us, here in Melbourne in the 1940s - by means of film, by creating images of reality, moving images, images to move mountains perhaps.

From *A Place to Live* (and the same shot is used also in *Prices and the People*), we see an image of an elderly man entering his shanty home. the image is projected onto a screen in the cinema, a frame within the frame.

ELIZABETH COLDICUTT

Ken Coldicutt, Bob Mathews and Gerry Harant knew that cinema was a form of art, at a time when the Hollywood monopoly masked in Australia the potential of cinema as an expressive medium.

Lights come up in the cinema and we dissolve through to a screen design with images of the main characters in the film and a gradually shifting series of still images from *These Are Our Children*.

NARRATOR

Ken Coldicutt taught at Camberwell Grammar where he established a film society and filmmaking groups among students, some of whom went on to make their own independent films. In the early 1980s with Gerry Harant and Joan Coxsedge he wrote and published Rooted in Secrecy, *an expose of the clandestine element of Australian politics.*

Bob Mathews went on to be a successful businessman in the fashion industry, building the Witchery chain. He remained a supporter of the Melbourne International Film Festival all his life and quietly contributed to the financing of a number of Australian independent films.

Elizabeth Coldicutt developed her career in teaching and continued her activism in community groups concerned with housing and in particular in support of refugees.

Gerry Harant does guest appearances on The Anarchist Hour *with Community Radio 3CR in Melbourne and writes for* Overland *magazine. He's the longest serving member of the Melbourne International Film Festival.*

A projection screen reflects a graphic 'exit', closing credits begin…

The Realist Film Association continued until the late 1950s. By then everything had changed: television had arrived and a commercial market had grown for art house cinema.

Activist filmmaking continued.

Curtains close and closing credits roll up.

Writer/Director	John Hughes
Editor/Co-director	Uri Mizrahi
Producers	John Hughes
	Philippa Campey
Screen Design/Animation	Uri Mizrahi
Composer	Martin Friedel
Camera	Kim Batterham,
	Amiel Courtin-Wilson,
	Michael Dillon, John Hughes,
	Cormac Lally, Uri Mizrahi,
	David Muir, Paul Oliver
Sound	Special thanks to
	Music and Effects, Melbourne,
	Emma Bortignon
	& Cynthia Mann
	& Huzzah Sound Sydney,
	Andrew Plain,
	Mike Jones, Damian Condusso
Voice Over	Bryan Brown, Nicos Lathouris,
	Deborah Mailman, Mark Rogers,
	Louise Smith, Andrew Wiseman
Sound Mix	Keith Thomas,
	Music and Effects, Melbourne
Colourist	Vincent Taylor,
	Complete Post, Melbourne
Post Production Facility	Blue Rose - U&A Editing
Legals	Karen Goodwin,
	Marshalls and Dent Lawyers
Production Accountant	Monika Gehrt
Transcripts	Anne Marie Allan
	& Netanela Mizrahi
Post Production Script	Anne Marie Allan

Special Thanks

Elizabeth Coldicutt, Gerry Harant, Sue Mathews, the Coldicutt Family, the Mathews Family, Angela O'Brien, Historian of the New Theatre, Melbourne, Philip Adams, Karin Altmann (AFC), Jason Benjamin (Melbourne University Archives), Audrey Blake, Jan Blake, John Cumming, Sharon Connolly, Phoebe Cutting, Graeme Cutts, Maryanne Doyle, June Factor, Pat Fiske, John Flaus, Courtney Gibson (ABC), Sofya Gollon, Cecil Grivas, Jodie Harris, Norma (Disher) Hawkins, Carl Johnston, Paula Kehoe, Peter Kennedy, David McKnight, Noga Mizrahi, Yukiko Abe Kruithof, Joanna Leahy (Performing Arts Museum), Belinda Mason, Joan Meltzer, David Muir, Don Munro, Eileen Naseby (FilmWorld), Nova Cinemas, Rita Parkinson (NFSA), Zsuzsi Szucs (NFSA), Charlotte Seymour (ABC), Carole Sklan, Neil Sharkey (NAA), Helen Tully (NFSA), Mark Tarpey, Steve Thomas (VCA), Sasha Trikojus, Stephen Wallace (AFC), Steve Warne (Film Victoria), David Vance, Deane Williams, Lucy Wright, Tom Zubrycki

Archival Sources

Audrey Blake, Jan Blake, Greg Coldicutt, Graeme Cutts, John Hughes, Angela O'Brien, Ed Schefferle, Sam de Silva, Deane Williams, The Arts Centre, Performing Arts Collection, Melbourne, Film World Australia, Mosfilm Cinema Concern, National Archives of Australia, National Film & Sound Archive, Noel Butlin Archive, ANU, Oral History Collection, National Library of Australia, State Library of Victoria, The University of Melbourne Archives,

Carl Vine:	'Chamber Music Vol. 2'
	'Inner World', 'String Quartet 3'
	courtesy of Tall Poppies Records
	Hal Leonard Music Publishers
Ross Edwards:	'Piano Concerto':
	Dennis Hennig, piano
	Queensland Symphony Orchestra
	Courtesy of ABC Classics
	BMG Music Publishing Australia
Executive Producer	ABC TV Arts,
	Amanda Duthie

With thanks
Music and Effects
ACMI
Developed & Produced with the assistance of National Film and Sound Archive
A Division of the Australian Film Commission
Australian Film Commission
Produced with the assistance of Australian Broadcasting Corporation
Produced & Developed with the assistance of Film Victoria
© Early Works and Film Victoria 2006

/G:MK   S E C R E T   (31)

Evaluation: ▮▮▮   ▮▮▮   Report No. 11543

▮▮▮

RFA Vic
Bob Beckner

Information: 15.11.57
Event: Recent
Report: 29.11.57

VICTORIA

REALIST FILM ASSOCIATION - PERSONALITIES

Bob BECKNER (u/i), aged approximately 40 years, is a member of the Realist Film Association and takes an active part in discussions at films shown by the Realist Film Association.

2.   Phillip ADAMS (u/i), aged approximately 19 years, is a new member of the Realist Film Association.

3.   Ray PERRY (u/i), aged approximately 16 years, is being taught projection work by Sid PRIOR (probably Sidney Ernest George PRIOR - VPF.2642).

INDEXED   30 JAN 1958

S. H.Q. (1)
Consumer Section H.Q. (3)
S, State (1)
B.1. State (as required)

S E C R E T

PHILLIP ADAMS

Phillip Adams, journalist and broadcaster, recalls his experience as a young teenager with Realist Film Association screenings at the New Theatre in Melbourne, and reflects on the 1960s 'renaissance' of the Australian film industry.

Phillip Adams: I left Eltham High School when I was about 15 to escape the tyranny of a crazed stepfather, and I got a job in an advertising agency in Melbourne called Briggs & James, and like most ad agencies, would you believe, in the 50s it was full of ex-Communists. In fact quite a few of the major agencies were run by ex-Coms. Why ex-Communists were working in the furnace holds of capitalism it was hard to explain but I think it was because they'd learnt propaganda skills as party members and these could be parlayed into a profession. All around the creative departments of advertising agencies and even at the top level you'd find people who you used to bump into at party meetings.

My first job was to deliver printing blocks to the *Melbourne Herald*, and on the way down to *The Herald* I'd drop off my columns, my film reviews, to *The Guardian*, the Communist newspaper. So in my CV I talk about starting my journalistic career with *The Guardian* and people think I mean the famous one in England, but I don't, I mean the Melbourne branch of *The Tribune*.

I had to pass a place called the New Theatre which was next to The Herald and Weekly Times, and I became curious about this. I went to a few screenings there and saw things like *Battleship Potemkin* and *The Childhood of Maxim Gorky*. And then wandering down the Yarra Bank one Sunday I heard some Communist speakers and thought, this is for me, this sounds good, so I went up and volunteered for active service. I became one of the few kids of my era who actually joined the Communist Party. In fact I was allowed to join underage by special dispensation. So suddenly I found my party job was writing film reviews for *The Guardian* and screening films at the Realist Film Association in the New Theatre.

My job was to stoke up the potbellied stove at nights at film screenings, sell a few tickets out the front, go upstairs to the little bio box where there was a couple of clapped-out Bell and Howell projectors, load up the movies. Then I would try to synchronise 78 recordings with the film, so as to give the few people sitting downstairs in this battered little cinema a full sensual experience. So I'd be trying to synchronise Shostakovich records, 78s, with the famous step sequence in Potemkin, and it was a great place to be.

I never got to university, but hanging around New Theatre, Realist Film, *The Guardian* and party meetings were a substitute for me, and through it I met extraordinary people. It does seem to me that that era for me, the 50s, that almost anyone who could think or feel seemed to be a member of the Communist Party. There was no real film industry at the time. The number of professional plays produced in Australia during the 50s could be counted on the fingers of two hands, literally, whereas the Realist movement was doing its best, the New Theatre movement was doing its best, the Australasian Book Society was doing its best to keep these arguments alive. Nowadays of course much art is really hard to distinguish from interior decoration, but then you were dealing with big issues, of war and peace particularly.

My first exposure to the idea that Australians could actually make films themselves came from this time. It came from the Wharfies Film Unit with these extraordinary documentaries on the life of wharfies, which I knew off by heart because I used to screen them night after night as a part of my Party and projectionist duties. We'd meet people like Cecil Holmes who were making films from Frank Hardy stories or Henry Lawson stories. So there was this subculture of defiant nationalistic, internationalistic arts activity happening around the New Theatre and around the Realist Film Association.

The industry had been pretty much derailed and destroyed in the 30s when the Americans and the Brits took over the distribution in the cinemas. So Australia's vibrant and energetic film industry which had been going for yonks, almost since day one, had pretty much petered out. But there were people like Cecil Holmes, identified with the Communist Party, who were trying to tell working class or radical stories, and miraculously managed to make films. God knows how they did it.

You'd had a huge amount of film activity in this country, and running on two lines; there was the cultural nationalist line right from day one where someone would be making a film on Ned Kelly, and down the road in another paddock there'd be someone making a film on Buffalo Bill. There were always these two ideas; one that you told your own stories and one that you told American stories. That stereophonic tradition continues, except these days one of the soundtracks is much louder than the other.

Quite a few of those of us involved in the RFA were also members of the Melbourne Film Society which became the largest film society in the world. And that had an effect on the Melbourne Film Festival which, in its category, was one of the largest film festivals in the world. So Melbourne picked up again with the film culture and out of that film culture came Tim Burstall and the filmmakers of the 60s, myself included, who were trying to make films on low budgets or no budgets, and to find an audience. So you can draw connections between that activity in the 60s which led to Barry Jones and I persuading John Gorton to do something about it, and those other activities in Melbourne. So if you pulled the RFA out of the sequence, I don't think it would have happened. I think it was quite an important stage in the sequence of events that got the film industry up and running again. But it's not recorded anywhere, it's not written about, it's not understood.

I wrote one sheet of paper, it was just one piece of paper, to Gorton on behalf of Barry Jones, Peter Coleman, oddly enough, and it said, 'We hold these truths to be self-evident,' a bit of a pun there, really. 'It's time to see our own landscapes, hear our own voices and dream our own dreams.' It was a cultural nationalist declaration, pretty much in the tradition of what we're talking about. And it persuaded Gorton, who was something of a cultural nationalist himself oddly enough, to press some of the buttons, and then of course Whitlam would then pick up and put real money behind these propositions. So we got our film school, we got our film funds going, and the rest is history.

But these days of course that impetus, that intensity of feeling has pretty much disappeared. The film industry is now dominated by the American industry. So that battle, the great battle for cultural nationalism is all but lost now, and I think that's a tragedy. I take no pleasure in seeing an endless succession of fine Australian actors queuing for their Oscars. In fact I wrote a piece not so long ago saying that I regarded Australians winning Oscars as being golden nails in the coffin of our industry. The industry existed, as far as I was concerned, for purposes of cultural identity, for national identity and for some sort of cultural and political engagement that is now almost totally absent.

There are still a few eccentrics… some Aboriginal filmmakers, for example, who are trying to tell their stories and tell them well, but out of every $100 spent at the box office in Australia, $93, $94 goes on an American film, leaving $5 or $6 for the entire rest of the world, Australia included. And really, the political will to ward this off is almost totally absent. The Labor Party doesn't seem to be much more concerned about it than the Libs. There's some arguments that we might be able to protect what's left of our industry, but the battle has been lost in the sense that young filmmakers, their first instinct is to become part of the great global juggernaut, and of course in film terms that simply means you plug into Los Angeles. Very sad. ■

DICK MASON

Richard 'Dick' Mason (1925 – 2002), director and producer in Australian documentary and drama talks about his career and recalls how he overcame the security blacklisting of filmmaker Cecil Holmes at Australia's Commonwealth Film Unit in the 1960s. Based on an audio interview with Dick conducted by John Hughes and Tom Zubrycki in 1982.

Dick Mason: I was a soldier in the Second World War. When I came back I just wanted to do something in the theatre. I was working as a backstage manager doing production, producing and amateur plays and things, and living… actually we were sleeping in the theatre.

Peter Finch got a job at a filming company called Ealing Studios, came out to do *Eureka Stockade*. That would have been in 1947, something like that. They came out to do the filming. He said to me, 'Do you want a job in the film as a wardrobe assistant. Can you sew?' I said, 'Yes, sure, I've sewed my buttons on in the army, I can sew.' My mind was blown! Cinema to me was just the Americans, cinema was overseas, it wasn't Australia, there wasn't any Australian cinema. I just had this view that you used to go along and be enthralled by Clark Gable and… we didn't get any European films, so just American films and British films.

I went and got my deferred pay and I formed a company, Opus Film Productions. Because I was working in the theatre and I was with, at that stage, a lot of friends in SORA, the Society of Realist Art, I decided to make a film called *An Introduction to Australian Art*. And I'd got three young artists, Bill Dobell, Russell Drysdale and a bloke called Roy Dalgarno, which is not bad, two out of three.

I realised in the process of making it that I didn't know anything about filmmaking. I had to learn. And there was nowhere to work and I'd really got smitten by the filmmaking bug, and there was no way to make money out of films because they cost a lot and there wasn't any way to get work.

But Professor Stout, who was associated with the AFI, the establishment of the Sydney Film Festival and the establishment of the AFI, saw the film at the screening at Sydney University. He was really nice to me and said, 'Look, you should meet Stanley Hawes.' I got this invitation and it was to work as a production assistant on a film with Lee Robinson. When that finished and I thought it's really terrific, you know, there was a question of whether I should be kept on or not. Stanley said, 'I think we ought to let that Dick Mason go,' and Lee Robinson said, 'Oh but he's been very good on the production.' But Stanley said, 'But he's a Catholic and we can't have any Catholics, we've got too many Catholics.' Stanley Hawes hated Roman Catholics and policemen and blood sports. His three great hates; blood sports, policemen and Roman Catholicism were the great hates, you see.

But Lee said, 'But he's not a Roman Catholic. His old man's a Baptist parson.' I was allowed to stay. My religion got me in, you see, or stopped me from being… if I'd been Roman Catholic I wouldn't be in the industry today probably.

Working on lots of films I learnt the craft. I was involved in the church, and the Home Mission Department said to me, would I like to make a film? I said, 'Yes.' I immediately thought of Cecil. At the time I met Cecil Holmes, Cecil Holmes couldn't get a job anywhere, he really was… things were crook, and he was the filmmaker who I admired, and I admired him most for *Three in One*, his second feature film, which is the three stories, and I thought was great. Here's a filmmaker much better, I felt, than myself and a filmmaker much better than most of the people I was working with, with skills and talents, and he couldn't get work for political reasons that was, to me, shocking. So I got Cecil, and Cecil and I made *Faces in the Sun*, a film about the Aborigines in Arnhem Land. It caused an incredible stir because it was really looking forward with concern about the dignity of the people and the right of the Aborigines to control themselves, to control… to have the land.

I wanted Cecil… I got a job at Film Australia. I think I was just a film director, which at Film Australia in the hierarchy you had no status, so I couldn't have given him a job, but I think he got an invitation to do a job. Jack Allen who claimed he was ASIO's representative, he went to Stanley Hawes and said, 'Look, I've been in touch with ASIO and you cannot employ Cecil Holmes, he's a Communist.' And that was it.

A mate of mine is an engineer and he's going to get a job that's connected with Defence, and he gives me as a reference for his security clearance. I went in to Stanley and I said, 'Look, I've got a meeting with security, and I'd like to check out on Cecil just to make sure that it's okay,' and Stanley went along with it. So these guys came and they did their business and I said, 'Look, I've got another thing to raise; we have a filmmaker, Cecil Holmes, and we'd like to employ him, and we'd just like to check out that it's okay, that there's no barrier to employing him.'

Well, this started a series of meetings in which these guys… and it boiled down that their proposition was that if Cecil Holmes told all his contacts, revealed all the contacts, he could then come and work, he'd be cleared, you see? So I went and told Cecil this, and I said, 'Mate, you can't do this.' He said, 'No, I can't do that.' So I went back and I said, 'No, there's nothing he's got to tell. What do we do now?' And they said, 'Oh well, we have to consult.' So this was going on, and I got jack of this, and then at this final meeting, final as far as I was concerned… I said, 'Look, I am now going to report to the Producer-in-Chief that it's okay to employ Cecil Holmes.' It's simple. I went in and told Stanley, 'Yes, it's fine, it's cleared.' ∎

DON MUNRO

Don Munro (1928 -2007) was devoted to Melbourne's New Theatre. Here he talks about what the theatre meant to him and what the 'New' achieved for Australian theatre. Based on an interview by John Hughes, shot by David Muir, 2005.

Don Munro: When I first came down from Ballarat to work in Melbourne, Sundays nights were… nothing on like there is now, and I happened to notice in the paper that there was this theatre in Flinders Street that was showing films on a Sunday night. Not only were they showing all these classic films but it was 'enter by donation' which, as a struggling worker boarding in Melbourne, that was a nice help too. So I finished up going just about every Sunday night, or every time they changed the program anyway, and got to know a number of people. Then one night one of these characters said, 'You're always here, why don't you join the film association?' And I said, 'Oh yeah, do you make films?' They said, 'Oh no, no, haven't made anything for ages.' And I said, 'I'm only interested in the acting side.' 'Ah well, you should join New Theatre.' And that's how I eventually got into the theatre, and that became a large part of my life. Almost every night of the week I was either rehearsing or performing. As my wife would say, I divorced her and joined the theatre.

'52 was my first play and I was with the theatre virtually until it disintegrated about two or three years ago. The last few years I've done one show every couple of years when someone rings me up and says, 'We really need an old man.' But my heart has always been with them. I'm surprised my wife put up with me really. I suppose her hands were full with the kids. It was a life… you were there at all times. With small kids it would be work all day and very often I'd go straight from work to the theatre because you wouldn't have time to go home. So it was four or five nights a week. Then when the show started it would be four nights a week, and towards the end of it you might be rehearsing the next one Monday and Tuesday and Sunday, so it could be seven nights a week.

Quite a proportion of the actors were professionals. There was no film industry as such at that stage, there was no television, and the theatre was… if you were lucky enough you got a small part playing against big stars from overseas in overseas plays. If you were a professional your main money-making was doing ads for radio or the odd radio play like Lux Radio Theatre or something like that.

I was unaware of how many but probably a third to half of the membership of the theatre were members of the Communist Party. It was very much part of the peace movement, pushing ideas which I certainly agreed with, even when I wasn't a member of the Party. I mean, I joined it later.

Ted Thompson and Dot Thompson, who were in the theatre, and Nicky and myself and a small baby which was the eldest went to Adelaide. We were followed the entire way across, where we stopped and what we did when we were there and… just amazing. And there was a Christmas BBQ in Melbourne and lots of theatre people and various other people turned up. Whether he was in a car out the front or in a house over the road or where I don't know, but he had a list of everyone who arrived, when they arrived, when they left, the whole BBQ. It was just amazing… God, tax payers are paying for this nonsense. If anyone wanted to know we would have told them who was there. It wasn't a political meeting, it was just a Christmas BBQ.

It usually gets bogged down in the politics, which I think you can't avoid that, it was a big part of the theatre. But the theatre's contribution to culture in Australia was important. Virtually there wouldn't have been any Australian theatre for… it might have come eventually but it wouldn't have come at the time it did if it wasn't for New Theatre. I suppose I wouldn't be saying we 'caused it' but we certainly were the first ones to be pushing it. If the theatre has done nothing else it's done that. ■

DOT THOMPSON

Dorothy 'Dot' Thompson (1914-2001) was a key figure at Melbourne's New Theatre. Here she speaks with oral historian Wendy Lowenstein about the 'New' in the 1930 and '40s. This is an edited version of an interview derived from the Oral History Collection, National Library of Australia.

Wendy Lowenstein: This is Wendy Lowenstein interviewing Dot Thompson… New Theatre in Melbourne, early 1993.

Dot Thompson: Radio was an enormous thing. 3AK used to run late sessions at night where you could go, and I wrote plays and performed in them, and did anything…

Wendy Lowenstein: And was it well paid?

Dot Thompson: You got a little money for it. It was more on the amateur style I suppose. Part of the job used to be to take someone's bets over the phone. That led me into New Theatre. So I go along and I see *Bury the Dead*. That was my first introduction to New Theatre, and I thought, well, this is the sort of thing that I'm interested in. I was absolutely astounded, I couldn't believe it.

Wendy Lowenstein: *Bury the Dead*, of course, by Irwin Shaw, was a very anti-war play. This was '38, obviously the war was coming.

Dot Thompson: I think it's one of the most important plays that's been written this century. Having seen the play and met these people… but I didn't actually… it was the following year, the end of the following year, it was in '39 I must have joined. I went along to New Theatre, got enough courage to go up and join up.

Wendy Lowenstein: Where were they?

Dot Thompson: They were in a place called Flannigan Lane.

Wendy Lowenstein: I remember that.

Dot Thompson: Flannigan Lane, 1939.

Wendy Lowenstein: You plunged into it.

Dot Thompson: Plunged into it, yes. Within five minutes I'm working backstage doing everything I possibly could. I met up with all these fascinating people, you know; actors and writers and artists. I was just taken aback that anybody could hop in and do anything.

Wendy Lowenstein: There was an enormous feeling of…

Dot Thompson: Oh yes, of friendliness and positive attitude to people. A 'we' rather than 'me' sort of an attitude, which doesn't exist… I think is one of the problems of today.

Wendy Lowenstein: Yes, I seem to remember that you were expected, if you were in one play, to do something like front-of-house at the next one. You were really expected to be in everything, weren't you, to be in…

Dot Thompson: Yes. Well, you naturally wanted to actually.

Wendy Lowenstein: It must have been very difficult. How did you fund the theatre? Were the actors paid?

Dot Thompson: Oh no, no, no, you only exist through your audience, what your audience paid to come and see the show.

Wendy Lowenstein: So New Theatre swept you up. When did you become aware of its political structure?

Dot Thompson: Oh it didn't take very long.

Wendy Lowenstein: The Party branch.

Dot Thompson: No, not so much that, it was the discussion on what was going on in the world, and that was highly significant. You were given books to read and you were reading madly of every book that came out. I don't remember any formal setup of a Communist Party branch of New Theatre ever. It was 1940 when I joined the Communist Party, when it was illegal, you see. I'd always do things at the best time.

Wendy Lowenstein: From what I remember, New Theatre was never a banned organisation like, say, the League of Young Democrats. It was never prescribed as being a Communist organisation, which was rather interesting. Can you imagine why?

Dot Thompson: Well, they probably didn't consider us very important.

Wendy Lowenstein: I seem to remember that the Communist Party branches and a lot of trade union branches actually ran theatre parties. I know in our Communist Party branch it was seen as a way of, something to take new contacts to.

Dot Thompson: At one stage it was decided not to put names on the program, for two reasons; one, to keep it so that we weren't working on a star system, but also to protect some people. People had to work under other names because there was blacklisting of a number of actors during that Cold War period.

Wendy Lowenstein: This is during the early 50s.

Dot Thompson: In the 50s, yes. The set designers in New Theatre I think were quite phenomenal. The earlier part was constructivist from the Russian constructivist and German constructivist movement, probably German more than the other. Very innovative approach to set design, very practical, very interesting, very effective.

Wendy Lowenstein: And New Theatre was always seen as being very left wing but in fact you were doing plays which are done today without… you were doing Moliere, you were doing classics, you were doing modern American…

Dot Thompson: Plays that didn't do well were the Australian plays. We discussed it at a meeting and decided that Australian plays should be given the best director and the best production so that people realised that the play had something, rather than making people say it wasn't properly done.

Wendy Lowenstein: They were pioneers in promoting Australian plays, giving room to Australian plays.

Dot Thompson: Yes, we were.

Wendy Lowenstein: I have never been in any organisation which was so exciting to be in.

Dot Thompson: I still have friendships now with people I knew back in the 40s. ■

MARGARET WALKER

Margaret Walker (1920-1996) established the Unity Dance Group that performed in factories and work sites, and contributed to New Theatre productions such as *White Justice* and *Spanish Village* in Melbourne during the 1940s. Here she talks about the Unity Dance Group and her years with the New Theatre. She dedicated her life to cultural diversity, dance and education. This is an edited version of an interview derived from the Oral History Collection, National Library of Australia.

Margaret Walker: I didn't really do any choreography until I joined the New Theatre and that was in 1944. I had the view by then that everybody should learn ballet, that everybody should know the music of the ballets and love it. It was quite a shock to get into theatre and the people in the productions that I put on had to make their own costume and they had to fit in their rehearsals with everything else that was going on, making the set and all of this. And I began to realise that outside the ballet school there was a great big world of dance, and outside the dance world there was a great big world.

There was a lot of things going on that in my childhood and youth I'd had no awareness of at all, but when I joined the New Theatre I was immediately confronted by these issues. And the thing that really affected me most was the sort of… once again, a broadening of the cultural values and the cultural experience. There were so many different strands brought together amongst the people in the New Theatre who at that time were a very interesting bunch. And I was involved in… asked to put on ballets in the reviews and so on. I got very involved in the theatre emotionally because what it did, it sort of brought through to me a social awareness that I hadn't had until then.

We established what we called the Unity Dance Group, this was about half a dozen girls and boys, and did lunch-hour concerts in factories and things like that. So we did some, and I soon realised you couldn't do ballet on a slippery floor in a factory canteen at lunchtime when no one was taking much notice of you anyway. You had to have a different kind of work, so I was immediately drawing on what I'd learnt from Borovansky, because Borovansky was a master of character dance and his wife was interested in classical ballet and it was the character work and the folk choreographies and things like that that were so valuable in this kind of area of dance.

In the Melbourne New Theatre we'd done a ballet there called *White Justice*, I think in 1946. A journalist by the name of Jim Crawford had been up at Port Hedland where there had been the first strike ever by Aboriginal station workers, and he came back and told us about this, and we used his experiences and the idea for a ballet set on the New Theatre stage showing the conditions on the station. And involved in that we had Aborigines from Fitzroy, the Onus family, and Eric was one of the lead dancers in this ballet. Eric's wife and other Aboriginals and their wives came, and came every night and rehearsed, they were really terrific. It was a very big thing, especially for these women, to get up and dance on the stage.

From *They Chose Peace* (Realist Film Unit, 1952): While the daily press carried on its campaign of slander, Australia's youth paper *Challenge* raised its voice in support of the carnival. Groups of young dancers and singers went out to tell the Australian workers the facts and ask for their support. Police were taken off essential duties of traffic and crime control to stop every expression of the carnival, but the dancing, singing and organising still went on.

Margaret Walker: The thing that I've learnt particularly through the New Theatre, where we had so many discussions on art and life, and there's a policy formulated in the theatre, and coming from, having got this through the ballet training I could see it then applied in society and I became interested in dance and its relationship to society. I got an understanding that, right, that folk dancing is something that people have always done and have always kept going in spite of efforts by the church or other people, the court, to stamp it out. ∎

REALIST FILM ASSOCIATION SCREENINGS: 1946–1958

Following is a list of Realist Film Association screenings held in Melbourne from 1946 to 1958. This material is sourced from Realist Film Association leaflets, correspondence and promotional materials between the years 1946 and 1958, with additional details for the films sourced from web-based film archives. Due to incomplete records this list cannot be considered exhaustive.

The screenings are categorised by year and, where the information is available, month, date or program theme. Where there has been no information available, the films have are in alphabetical order.

Some films have not been archived or are only partially documented (re: director, producer, production country, and year produced). Therefore:

An * before a listing indicates that it has not been possible to find all the bibliographical information for a film.

A # before a listing indicates that the details of the film require verification.

Unless indicated otherwise all of the films listed were screened at the New Theatre, Melbourne.

Compiled by: John Hughes, Lucy Wright, Lucy Demant

GLOSSARY

GPO: General Post Office

NFB: National Film Board

RFA: Realist Film Association

RFU: Realist Film Unit

UK: United Kingdom

USA: United States of America

WWF: Waterside Workers' Federation

REALIST FILM UNIT SCREENINGS 1946

The following films were screened mainly in the New Theatre in Melbourne, however in addition to these 'in 1946, 215 [non-theatrical] shows were given to audiences totalling 21,000… [in]… schools, youth clubs, trade unions… [and not only in]… Melbourne, also Geelong, Ballarat, Healesville, Yarra Junction, Yarram, Sale, Mirboo, Maffra, Wonthaggi' (RFU Circular, January 1947).

400 Film Stars. RFU. Footage of Eureka Youth League Christmas Holiday Camp. Silent (Australia), 1946.
69th Parallel. Belayev & Oshurkov. G.F.D. (USSR), 1940.
**A Better Tomorrow*. Dir. Alexander Hammid (USA), 1945.
**A Place to Live*. RFU. Silent (Australia), 1946.
Border Weave. Dir. John Lewis Curthoys. Central Office of Information (UK), 1942.

Charlie Chaplin, silent film season (titles unknown).
**China Strikes Back*. (People's Republic of China), 1944.
Crainquebille. Dir. Jacques Feyder. Films A. Legrand. Silent (France), 1922.

Documentary season: China, Czechoslovakia, Yugoslavia.
Fighting Lady. Dir. Carlos F. Borcosque. Fanchon Royer Pictures (USA), 1935.
Grass: A Nations Battle for Life. Dir. Richard Carver. Famous Players-Lasky Corporation. Silent (USA), 1925.
Indonesia Calling. Dir. Joris Ivens. Prod. for the Waterside Workers' Federation of Australia. Australasia Productions (Australia), 1946 (unofficially banned 1946).
La Kermesse Heroique. Dir. Jacques Feyder. Films Sonores Tobis (France), 1935.

Mack Sennett, silent film season.
Metropolis. Dir. Fritz Land. Prod. Erich Pommer. UFA (Germany), 1927.
No Greater Love. Dir. Fridrikh Ermler. Alma Ata Studio (USSR), 1943.
North Sea. Dir. Harry Watt. GPO Film Unit (UK), 1938.
Spring Song. Dir. Aleksandr Ivanovsky. Gosudarstvenii Komitet Po Kinematografii (USSR), 1941.
Season of NFB productions (Canada).
Ten Days that Shook the World. Dir. Sergei Eisenstein. Soukino. Silent (USSR), 1927.
The City. Dir. Ralph Steiner. Pare Lorentz & Willard Van Dyke. American Documentary Films Inc. (USA), 1939:
The True Glory. Dir. Garson Kanin. Ministry of Information (UK/USA), 1945.
The Valley of the Tennessee. Dir. Alexander Hammid. USA Office War Infomation (USA), 1944.
The White Hell of Pitz Palu. Dir. Wilhelm Pabst. Sokal-Film GmbH. Silent (Germany), 1929.
Three Waltzes. Dir. Ludwig Berger. SOFROR (France), 1938.
World of Plenty. Dir. Paul Rotha. Paul Rotha Productions (UK), 1943.
**Youth Plans and its Future*. RFU (Australia), 1946.

REALIST FILM UNIT SCREENINGS 1947

**A Night of Corn*. Silent.
Behind the Screen. Dir. Charlie Chaplin. USA Mutual Film Corporation (USA), 1916.
**Corporal Jim's Ward*. Irving Cummings.
**Czechoslovakia*.
**Eternal Prague*. Dir. Jiri Weiss (UK), 1940.
Faust. Dir. F. W. Murnau. Universum Film. Silent (Germany), 1926.
Film and Reality. Dir. Cavalcanti and Ernest Lindgren. National Film Library (Britain), 1942.
**In My Beginning*. RFU (Australia), 1947.
Indonesia Calling. Dir. Joris Ivens. Prod. for the Waterside Workers' Federation of Australia. Australasia Productions (Australia), 1946.
**Man, One Family*. Dir. Ivor Montagu (UK), 1946.
**May Day Demonstrations: Sydney, Melbourne, Adelaide*. RFU (Australia), 1947.
Men of Rochdale. Dir. Compton Bennett. Scottish Co-operative Wholesale Society (UK), 1944.
Metropolis. Dir. Fritz Land. Prod. Erich Pommer. UFA (Germany), 1927.
Othello (there are two possible records for this film):
1. **Othello*. David McCane (UK), 1946.
2. **Othello*. Max Mack. Silent (Germany), 1918.
**Our Country*
Out of the Ruins. Dir. Nickolas Read. NFB (Canada), 1946.
**Single-Shot Parker*. Dir. E. A. Martin (USA), 1917.
**Prices and the People*. RFU (Australia), 1948.
Season of recent films of the NFB (Canada).
Season of Charlie Chaplin 2-reelers.
Ten Days that Shook the World. Dir. Sergei Eisenstein. Soukino. Silent (USSR), 1927.
**The Battle for the Ukraine*.
**The Bridge*. Dir. J. D. Chambers (UK), 1946.
The Covered Wagon. Dir. James Cruze. Famous Players-Lasky Corporation (USA), 1923.
The Lost World. Dir. Harry Hoyt. First National Pictures (USA), 1925.
**The Slums Are Still With Us*. RFU (Australia), 1947.
**These Are Our Children*. RFU (Australia), 1946.

REALIST FILM UNIT / ASSOCIATION SCREENINGS 1948[1]

GENERAL SCREENINGS[2]
Battleship Potemkin. Dir. Sergei Eisenstein. First Studio Goskin. Silent (USSR), 1925.
Children on Trial. Jack Lee. Crown Film Unit (UK), 1946.
Cumberland Story. Dir. Humphrey Jennings. Crown Film Unit (UK), 1947.

---

1   The Realist Film Association, incorporating the RFU, was formed in 1948.
2   Some films listed here under general screenings may have been screened as part of themed programs.

Diary for Timothy. Dir. Humphrey Jennings. Crown Film Unit (UK), 1945.
*Face of Britain. Dir. Paul Rotha (UK), 1935.
Grass: A Nations Battle for Life. Dir. Richard Carver. Famous Players-Lasky Corporation (USA), 1925.
*Mongolia. Bolod Nimintsiguit (USSR), 1945.
Mother (there are two possible records for this film):
1. **Mother*. Vsevolod Pudovkin. Silent (USSR),1926.
2. *Mother*. Dir. James Leo Meehan. R-C Pictures (USA), 1927.
*Nanook of the North. Dir. and Prod. Robert Flaherty (Canada), 1921.
North Sea. Dir. Harry Watt. GPO Film Unit (UK), 1938.
*Othello. Dir. David McCane (UK), 1946.
Power and the Land. Dir. Joris Ivens. United States Film Service (USA), 1940.
Samurun. Dir. Ernst Lubitsch. PAGU (Germany), 1920.

JULY PROGRAM

Season of Eastern European Animation
*Glimpses of Soviet Science.
*Little Red Riding Hood.
*Puppet Theatre.
*The Christmas Tree. Russian children's animation.

AUGUST PROGRAM

Chaplin season: August 22
Shanghaied. Dir. Charlie Chaplin. Essanay Film Manufacturing Company. Silent (USA), 1915.
The Champion. Dir. Charlie Chaplin. Essanay Film Manufacturing Company. Silent (USA), 1915.

Israeli season: August 8
*Assignment Tel-Aviv. Comm: Quentin Reynolds. Zionist Federation (UK), 1948.
House in the Desert. Dir. Ben Oyserman and Joseph Krumgold. Prod. Norman Lourie. Palestine Film Production Ltd. United Palestinian Appeal (Israel), 1948.

REALIST FILM ASSOCIATION SCREENINGS 1949

Children on Trial. Dir. Jack Lee. Crown Film Unit (UK), 1946.
Italian Straw Hat. Dir. René Clair. Prod. Alexandre Kamenka. Films Albatros (France), 1927.
Metropolis. Dir. Fritz Lang. Prod. Erich Pommer. UFA (Germany), 1927.
Mother (there are two possible records for this film):
1. **Mother*. Vsevolod Pudovkin. Silent (USSR), 1926.
2. *Mother*. Dir. James Leo Meehan. R-C Pictures (USA), 1927.
*Nanook of the North. Dir. and Prod. Robert Flaherty (Canada), 1921.

*Rhythm of the City. Dir. Arne Sucksdorff (Sweden), 1947.
Siegfried. Dir. Fritz Lang. Decla-Bioscop AG. Silent (Germany), 1924.
The Birth of a Nation. Dir. David. W. Griffith. David. W. Griffith Corp. (USA), 1915.
*The Blue Angel. Dir. Josef von Sternberg (Germany), 1920.
*The Cabinet of Dr Caligari. Dir. Robert Wiene. Silent. (Germany), 1951.
*The Last Laugh. F.W. Murnau. Silent (Germany), 1924.
The River. Dir. Pare Lorentz. Farm Security Administration (USA), 1937.
*The Seashell and the Clergyman. Germaine Dulac and Antanin Artaud (France), 1928.
The World is Rich. Dir. Paul Rotha. Films of Fact (UK), 1947.
Thy Soul Shall Bear Witness. Dir. Victor Sjöström. Svensk Filmindustri (Sweden), 1921.
Turksib. Dir. Victor Turin. Vostokkino (USSR), 1929.

REALIST FILM ASSOCIATION SCREENINGS 1950

During 1950 the Realist Film Association screened 27 programs, 118 screenings, with an overall audience of 11,328. Beyond the New Theatre they organised another 163 screenings on behalf of other organisations to a total audience of 10,340 people (RFA Annual Report, December 1950).

A Dialectics of Cinema program of screenings and lectures, based on writings of Sergei Eisenstein and Vsevelod Pudovkin, was conducted by K. J. Coldicutt over several weeks; this may have been the first cinema studies course conducted in Australia.

GENERAL SCREENINGS

No Greater Love. Dir. Frederick Ermler. Alma Ata Studios (USSR), 1943.
General Line (The Old and the New). Dir. Sergei M. Eisenstein. Soukino (USSR), 1929.
Tanya. Dir. G.V. Alexandrov. Mosfilm (USSR), 1942.
Warning Shadows. Dir. Arthur Robinson. PAN Film. Silent (USSR), 1923.

APRIL PROGRAM

Evolution of Cinema Program: April 19–23
*Camera. Prod. Roger Leenhardt (UK), 1947.
*Drama among the Puppets. Dir. Émile Cohl. Animation (France), 1908.
Edgar Allan Poe. Dir. D. W. Griffiths. American Mutoscope & Biograph (USA), 1909.
*Evolution of the Motion Picture. Comm: J. Stuart Blackton (USA), 1947.
Modern Brigandage. Dir. Ferdinand Zecca. Pathé Cinéma (France),1905.

The Great Train Robbery. Dir. Edwin S. Porter. Edison Manufacturing Company (USA), 1903.
**The Life of Charles Peace*. Dir. William Haggar (UK), 1905.

MAY PROGRAM

Drama and Ballet Program: May 21 – 23
**Julius Caesar*.
**Prague Dramatic School* (Czechoslovakia).
**Steps of the Ballet*.

JUNE PROGRAM

The Spanish Earth. Dir. Joris Ivens. Contemporary Historians. Spanish Adaptation (Spain), 1937.
Turksib. Dir. Victor Turin. Vostokkino (USSR), 1929.

SEPTEMBER PROGRAM

General screenings
**In My Beginning*. RFU (Australia), 1947.
**Kazakhstan* (USSR).
Papworth Village Settlement. Dir. James Carr. World Wide Pictures (UK), 1946.
The Frazers of Cabot Cove. Dir. Humphrey Swingler. Greenpark Productions (Canada), 1949.

Australian program
Around a Gumtree. Dir. David Billcock. Shell Film Unit (Australia), 1949.
Cane Cutters. Dir. Hugh McInnes. NFB (Australia), 1948.
Gold Town. Dir. Maslyn Williams. NFB (Australia), 1949.
Prices and the People. Dir. Bob Mathews. RFU (Australia), 1948.
Seaside Holiday. Janice Moore. Country Roads Board. Home movie (Australia) 1947.
Steady As She Goes. Dir. John Kingsford-Smith. Kingcroft Australia (Australia), 1949.
The Meeting Place. Dir. Catherine Duncan. NFB (Australia), 1947.

Israeli program
**Histadrut. Builder of a Nation* (Israel).
**Homecoming*. (Israel), 1949.
**Memorandum on a Victory*. (Israel).
Tomorrow is a Wonderful Day. Dir. Helmar Lerski. Hadassah (Israel/Palestine), 1947.

Charlie Chaplin program
Behind the Screen. Dir. Charlie Chaplin. USA Mutual Film Corporation (USA), 1916.
Easy Street. Dir. Charlie Chaplin. Lone Star Corporation. Silent (USA), 1917.
The Pawnshop. Dir. Charlie Chaplin. Lone Star Corporation. Silent (USA), 1916.
The Tramp. Dir. Charlie Chaplin. Essanay Film Manufacturing Company. Silent (USA), 1915.

OCTOBER PROGRAM

General screenings
No Greater Love. Dir. Frederick Ermler. Alma Ata Studios (USSR), 1943.
**The Day Begins*. Dir. Mack Sennett. Charlie Chaplin (USA), 1914.
The Rink. Charlie Chaplin. Lone Star Studios. Silent (USA), 1914/1916.

Australian program
Antarctic Adventure. Jack S. Allan. NFB (Australia), 1948.
Bushfire Brigade. Eric Thompson. NFB (Australia), 1949.
Namatjira the Painter. Dir. Stanley Hawes and Lee Robinson. NFB (Australia), 1947.
The Lighthouse Keeper. Lionel Trainor. NFB (Australia), 1949.
The Valley is Ours. Dir. John Heyer. NFB (Australia), 1948.

Canadian program
Bluebloods of Canada. Dir. Michael Spencer. NFB (Canada), 1948.
Cadet Rousselle. Dir. George Dunning. NFB (Canada), 1947.
Children's Concert. Dir. Gudrun. NFB (Canada), 1949.
Ski Skills. Bernard Devlin and Roger Blais. NFB (Canada), 1946.

NOVEMBER PROGRAM

General screenings
Ten Days that Shook the World. Dir. Sergei Eisenstein. Soukino. Silent (USSR), 1927.

Australia-Soviet house program
Drifters. Dir. John Grierson. Empire Marketing Board (UK), 1929.
**Glory to Labour*. Reels 1, 4 & 7 (USSR).
**The Young Guard*. Dir. Gerasimov (USSR), 1948.
This Was Japan (there are two possible records for this film):
1. **This Was Japan*. Cinesound Review (Australia), 1945.
2. *This Was Japan*. Dir. Basil Wright. Crown Film Unit (UK), 1945.
Neuro-Psychiatry. Dir. Michael Hankinson and Basil Wright. Crown Film Unit (UK), 1943.

DECEMBER PROGRAM

Films on children's education program
Lessons in Living. Dir. Bill MacDonald. NFB (Canada), 1944.
School in the Mailbox. Dir. Stanley Hawes. NFB (Australia), 1947.
**Soviet School Child*. Central Film Studio (USSR), 1940.
**Their Small World*. (Czechoslovakia).
**The Three A's*. (England).
**Wilson Dam School*. (USA).

Films on child health program
RFU for British Ministry of Information 1945-51 (UK): *Your Children and You*; *Your Children's Ears*; *Your Children's Eyes*; *Your Children's Teeth*; *Your Children's Meals* and *Your Children's Sleep*.

Films on pictorial art program
*Hermitage Museum. Lentekh Film Studio (USSR), 1939.
*In the Country of Thyl Ulenspiegel. (Belgium).
Third Dimension. Dir. Laurence Hyde. NFB (Canada), 1947.
Van Gogh. Dir. Alain Resnais. Panthéon Productions (France), 1948.
West Wind. Dir. Graham McInnes. NFB (Canada), 1944.
1848. Dir. Victoria Spiri Mercanton and Margeurite de la Mure. Coopérative Générale du Cinéma Francais (France), 1949.

Maya Deren program
*At Land. Dir. Maya Deren (USA), 1944.
*Meshes of the Afternoon. Dir. Maya Deren and Alexander Hammid (USA), 1943.
*Ritual in Transfigured Time. Dir. Maya Deren (USA), 1946.
*Study in Choreography for Camera. Dir. Maya Deren (USA), 1945.

REALIST FILM ASSOCIATION SCREENINGS 1951

During 1951, the Realist Film Association presented at New Theatre 35 different programs in 132 screenings, reaching audiences totalling 14,335. In addition [the RFA] screened 164 programs for other organisations, reaching a total audience of 12,234 (*Realist Film News*: April 1952, Realist Film Association pamphlet).

JANUARY PROGRAM
Atom at the Crossroads. Dir. Cenek Duba. Prod. Bratri V Triku. Prague Puppet and Cartoon Studio. Animation (Czechoslovakia), 1947.
Behind the Screen. Dir. Charlie Chaplin. USA Mutual Film Corporation (USA), 1916.

January 19–28 (six screenings):
The Battle of Russia. Why We Fight Series. Dir. Joris Ivens, Anato le Litvak and Frank Capra, U.S. Office of War Information (USA), 1943.

January 22: discussion group 'Czech Short Films'.

January 31 – February 18 (15 screenings):
Krakatit. Dir. Otakar Vavra. The Otaker Vavra – Feix Unit, (Czechoslovakia), 1947.

FEBRUARY PROGRAM

General screenings
February 25: *Battle for the Ukraine*. Dir. J. Solnseva and J. Avdeenko. Central and Ukrainian Newsreel Studios (Ukraine), 1943.
February 25: **The Greatest Day of the Sokol Slet*. Documentary Section Czechoslovak State Films (Czechoslovakia).
February 26: discussion group 'Krakatit'.

Theatre
February 24 – March 17: *Thirty Pieces of Silver*. Howard Stern, New Theatre.

MARCH PROGRAM

General screenings
Film and Reality. Dir. Cavalcanti and Ernest Lindgren. National Film Library (Britain), 1942.

'Films on the Aborigines' series: March 4
Namtjira the Painter. Dir. Stanley Hawes and Lee Robinson. NFB (Australia), 1947.
*Tjurunga. NFB (Australia), 1946.
Walkabout. Dir. Charles Mountford. NFB (Australia), 1946.

International women's program: March 8, 11
Tanya. Dir. G.V. Alexandrov. Mosfilm (USSR), 1942.
Children Must Learn. Dir. Willard Van Dyke. Educational Film Institute of New York University (USA), 1940.
*Prague Dramatic School (Czechoslovakia).

Workers' Art Festival: Labor Day weekend March 9–12
Organising Bodies: Eureka Art Group, New Theatre, Unity Dance Group, Realist Writers and Realist Film Association

MARCH – APRIL PROGRAM
March 28 – April 8: *Spring*. G.V. Alexandrov. Sovexportfilm. Mosfilm (USSR), 1947.
March 28 – April 8: **Youth Peace Warriors*.
March 28 – April 8: *1848*. Dir. Victoria Spiri Mercanton and Margeurite de la Mure. Coopérative Générale du Cinéma Francais (France), 1949.
April 11 – 29: **The Young Guard* (Parts 1 and 2). Dir. Sergei Gerasimov (USSR), 1947.

MAY PROGRAM

May Day program of trade union films: May 6
Battle for Coal. Dir. Leonid Lukov. Mosfilm. Czech State Film (Czechoslovakia), 1951.
Coal Dust. Edmund Allison. RFU. The Australian Miners' Federation (Australia), 1945.
Fighting Back. Dir. Cecil William Holmes. The New Zealand Carpenters' Union (New Zealand), 1949.
Indonesia Calling. Dir. Joris Ivens. Prod. for the Waterside Workers' Federation of Australia. Australasia Productions (Australia), 1946.
*May Day Melbourne: 1946-48-50. RFU (Australia).

Pursuit of Happiness. Dir. Rudy Burckhardt. Sponsored by U.S. Meatworkers Union (USA), 1940.
Sorting it Out: A Trade Union at Work. Dir. Philip Leacock. RFU (UK), 1948.

General screenings: May 13
69th Parallel. Dir. V. Belyaev and M. Oshurkov. Central Newsreel Studios (USSR), 1942.
Screenings of British documentaries – titles unknown.

French program: May 20
Chosen from:
Islam. Dir. Georges dir Régnier. Films J.K. Raymond-Millet (France), 1950.
Journal of Resistance. Comm. by Pierre Blanchar. Liberation Committee of the French Cinema (France), 1945.
La Rose et le Reseda. Dir. André Michel. Comm. by Jean-Louis Barrault. French Cinema Co-operative (France), 1947.
Pacific 231. Dir. Jean Mitry. Tadié Cinéma (France), 1949.
The Scientific Work of Louis Pasteur. Dir. Georges Rouquier. Ciné-Franc (France), 1947.
Screening of other French films – titles unknown.

American program: May 27
Chosen from:
*A Place to Live. Dir. Irving Lerner (USA), 1941.
Boundary Lines. Dir. Phillip Stapp. Prod. Julien Bryan. Animation. International Film Foundation (USA), 1947.
Brotherhood of Man. Dir. Robert Cannon. Animation. United Auto Workers (USA), 1945.
**F.D.R.* (USA).
The City (there are two possible records for this film):
1. *The City*. Dir. Ralph Steiner and Willard Van Dyke. American Documentary Films (USA), 1939.
2. *The City*. Dir. R. William Neill. Fox Film Corportation (USA), 1926.
Children Must Learn. Dir. Willard Van Dyke. Educational Film Institute of New York University (USA), 1940.
Screening of other American Films – titles unknown.

General screenings: May 28
Rubens. Dir. Paul Haesaerts and Henri Storck. Belgian Ministries of Education and Communication (Belgium), 1949.

MAY – JUNE PROGRAM

General screenings[3]
Daughters of China. Dir. Zifeng Ling and Qiang Zhai. China Northeast Film Studio (People's Republic of China), 1949.
Kameradschaft. Dir. G.W. Pabst. Neo Film (Germany and France), 1931.
New Babylon. Dir. Grigori Kozintzev and Leonid Trauberg. Sovkino (USSR), 1929.
**Peace Shall Conquer the World*.

The End of St. Petersburg. Dir. Vsevolod Pudoukin. Mezhrabpom Russ Studio (USSR), 1927.
Waxworks. Dir. Paul Leni. Neptun-Film (Germany), 1924.

Swedish and Danish program: June 3
Good Mothers. Dir. Carl Dreyer. Prod. Mogens Skot-Hansen. Nordisk Film (Denmark), 1942.
Health for Denmark. Dir. Torben Anton Svendsen. Palladium. Danish Government Film Committee (Denmark and UK), 1947.
**People's Holiday*. Social Denmark Series (Denmark).
Rhythm of the City. Dir. Arne Sucksdorff. Svensk Filmindustri (Sweden), 1947,
Shaped by Danish Hands. Dir. Hagen Hasselbalch. Minerva Film (Denmark), 1947.
The Corn is in Danger. Dir. Hagen Hasselbalch. Nordisk Film (Denmark), 1945.
*The Foal.
Seventh Age. Dir. Torben Anton Svendsen. Palladium (Denmark), 1947.
**Wind from the West*. Dir. Arne Sucksdorff (Sweden), 1942.

Czechoslovakian program: June 10
Chosen from
**Dances of Valassko*.
**From Smoke and Dust*.
**The Night of February 28. 1948*.
**The New Constitution of Czechoslovakia*. British Czech Friendship League.
**Thirtieth Year of Czechoslovakia*. British Czech Friendship League.
**2 Mr Prokouk Puppet Films* (unknown titles). # Dir. Karel Zeman.

Israeli program: June 17
House in the Desert. Dir. Ben Oyserman and Joseph Krumgold. Prod. Norman Lourie. Palestine Film Production Ltd. United Palestinian Appeal (Israel), 1948.
*State in Action.
The Day has Come. Dir. Shmuel Schweig. Carmel Productions (Israel), 1950.

General screenings
From June 20 (for fifteen nights): *Son of the Regiment*. Dir. Y. Vasilchikov. Soyusdetfilm Studio (USSR), 1946.
*Glory to Labor (USSR), 1949.

Classes
Beginners and refreshers projectionist classes.

JULY PROGRAM

Five delegates represented the Realist Film Association at the Berlin World Youth Festival. Two delegates also attended the July 14–29 VI International Film Festival in Czechoslovakia.

---

[3] While these screenings were programmed due to incomplete records we cannot determine whether or not the films were actually shown.

AUGUST – SEPTEMBER PROGRAM

French and French-Canadian films: August 12
Art Survives the Times. English commentary.
Chants Populaires No.6. Dir. Norman McLaren. NFB. Animation (Canada), 1944.
Factories, Mines and Waterways. Earth and Peoples Series. Dir. John Ferno. Louis de Rochemont Associates.
Islam. Dir. Georges Régnier. J.K. Raymond-Millet (France), 1950.
La Rose et le Reseda. Dir. André Michel. Comm. by Jean-Louis Barrault. French Cinema Co-operative (France), 1947.
Sondeurs D'Abimes. Dir. Marcel I Chac. Coopérative Des Artisians d'Art Du Cinéma (France), 1943.
The Acadians. Haridix. NFB. English commentary (Candada), 1947.

Discussion nights:
August 14: 'Ken Coldicutt's script for youth film'.
August 28: 'The Fall of Berlin'.
September 11: 'Kameradschaft'.
September 25: 'Realist Films v. Hollywood'.

General screenings
August 19–September 2: *Kameradschaft*. Dir. G.W. Pabst. Neo Film (Germany and France), 1931.
September 7–9: *Slovak Pastures* and other films from Czechoslovakia (unknown titles).
September 7–9: *Steel Road*. Dir. V. Bahna (Czechoslovakia), 1950.
September 14–16: *Nanook of the North*. Dir. and Prod. Robert Flaherty (Canada), 1921.
September 21–23: *Battleship Potemkin*. Dir. Sergei Eisenstein. First Studio Goskin. Silent (USSR), 1925.
September 28–30: *On Stage*. NFB. Physical Fitness Division, Department of National Health (Canada), 1950.
September 28–30: *Prague Dramatic School* (Czechoslovakia).
September 28–30: *The Lady of the Camellias*. Dir. André Calmettes and Henri Pouctal. Film d'Art. Silent (France), 1910.
September 28–30: # *Two Chinese Dances*. USA China Film Enterprises.

OCTOBER PROGRAM

General screenings
October 7 & 14: *The Cabinet of Dr Caligari*. Dir. Robert Wiene. Silent. (Germany), 1951.
October 21 & 28: *No Greater Love*. Dir. Frederick Ermler. Alma Ata Studios (USSR), 1943.

DECEMBER PROGRAM

General screenings: December 2–9
Berlin Youth Festival. DEPA: East German Film Production Corporation (East Germany), 1951.
The River. Dir. Pare Lorentz. United States Department of Agriculture (USA), 1937.
The Spanish Earth. Dir. Joris Ivens. Contemporary Historians. Spanish Adaptation (Spain), 1937.

New British films: December 16, 23, 30
This Modern Age: Antarctic Wale Hunt. This Modern Age (UK), 1947.
As Old as the Hills. Dir. Allan Crick. Prod. John Halas. Technicolour Cartoon. Halas & Batchelor (UK), 1950.
Berth 24. Dir. J.B.Holmes. Prod. Edgar Anstey. British Transport Films (UK), 1950.
This Modern Age: Education for Living. Prod. Sergei Nolbandov. This Modern Age (UK), 1949.
Family Portrait. Dir. Humphrey Jennings. Prod. Ian Dalrymple. Wessex Film Productions (UK), 1950.
Festival in London. Dir. Philip Leacock. Prod. Frederick Wilson. Crown Film Unit (UK), 1951.
Life in her Hands. Dir. Philip Lencock. Prod. Frederick Wilson. Crown Film Unit (UK), 1951.
Out of True. Dir. Philip Lencock. Crown Film Unit (UK).
The Dancing Fleece. Dir, Frederic Wilson. Crown Film Unit (UK), 1950.
The Undefeated. Dir. Paul Dickson. Prod. James Carr. World Wide Pictures (UK), 1950.
This Modern Age: Thoroughbreds for the World. This Modern Age (UK), 1946.

REALIST FILM ASSOCIATION SCREENINGS 1952

New Theatre screenings and audiences increased in 1952 'in spite of the economic situation in Australia… screenings for 1952 numbered 162, an increase of 36 over 1951 and of 53 over 1950. The audiences increased from 11,328 in 1950 and 14,517 in 1951 to 21,515 in 1952. We held 185 screenings outside the New Theatre in 1952. A total of 14,888 persons attended them, an increase of 2654 over 1951' (*Realist Film News*: February – March 1953, Realist Film Association pamphlet, 3-4).

JANUARY PROGRAM

General screenings: January 6, 13, 18-20
Let's See. Dir. Robert Lapresle. Merton Park.
New Town. Dir. John Halas. Prod. Joy Batchelor. Halas and Batchelor. Animation (UK), 1948.
Scotch Whisky. Dir. Phillip Gee. British Movietonews (UK), 1947.
Vladimir Ilyich Lenin. Dir. V. Belyaev and M. Romm. Central Documentary Film Studios (USSR), 1948.

General Screenings: January 25–27
Peace Will Win. Dir. Joris Ivens. Trans. Ralph Bond. Film Polski (Poland), 1950.
The Undefeated. Dir. Paul Dickson. Prod. James Carr. World Wide Pictures (UK), 1950.

Olinda Film Festival: January 25–28
Organised by the Federation of Victorian Film Societies in conjunction with the Annual Convention of the Australian Council of Film Societies.

FEBRUARY PROGRAM

General screenings
New Fighters Will Arise. Dir. Otakar Vavra. Czechoslovak State Films (Czechoslovakia), 1950.

General screenings: February 1-3
Hold the Land. Dir. Geoffrey F. Collings. Prod. Geoffrey Bell. NFB (Australia), 1949.
Vladimir Ilyich Lenin. Dir. V. Belyaev and M. Romm. Central Documentary Film Studios (USSR), 1948.
Wordsworth Country. Dir. Derek Mayne. Prod. Frank Wells. Gaumont-British Instructional (UK), 1950.

Chinese Film Festival
February 4–8: *Daughters of China* (Zhong Hua nu er). Dir. Zifeng Ling and Qiang Zhai. China Northeast Film Studio (People's Republic of China), 1949.
February 11–15: *The White Haired Girl*. Dir. Pu Wang and Hua Shui. China Northeast Film Studio (People's Republic of China), 1950.
February 18–22: *Liberated China*. Dir. Svetozarou Kuznetsov. Gorky Moscow Cine Studios (USSR in collaboration with the People's Republic of China), 1950.

General screenings: February 8–10
Daybreak in Udi. Dir. Terry Bishop. Crown Film Unit (UK), 1949.
This Modern Age: Education for Living. Prod. Sergei Nolbandov. This Modern Age (UK), 1949.
Peace Will Win. Dir. Joris Ivens. Trans. Ralph Bond. Film Polski (Poland), 1950.
Your Children: Your Children's Play. Dir. Brian Smith. RFU (UK), 1951.

General screenings: February 15–17
*Journey for Peace.
*Rytmus (Rhythm). Dir. Jirí Lehovec. (Czechoslovakia), 1941.
The World is Rich. Dir. Paul Rotha. Films of Fact (UK), 1947.
*Toyland Revolt. Animated Puppet Film (Czechoslovakia), 1949.

General screenings: February 22–24
Animated Cartoons: **The Toy that Grew Up*. Dir. Roger Leenhardt (USA), 1947.
*This Modern Age: Home and Beauty. This Modern Age (UK), 1947.
Krakatit. Dir. Otakar Vavra. The Otaker Vavra – Feix Unit (Czechoslovakia), 1947.
This is Britain: Love of Books. Dir. Cyril Frankel. Crown Film Unit (UK), 1951.

Screening and Discussion on film production: February 24[4]
Subject: The origins and development of cinema: technical, economic, and social.
Films chosen from: *Film and Reality*; *Birth of a Motion Picture Camera*; *Animated Cartoons*: *The Toy that Grew Up* and *March of the Movies*.

MARCH PROGRAM

General screenings: March 2
Film and Reality. Dir. Alberto Cavalcanti and Ernest Lindgren. National Film Library (UK), 1942.
*Rhythm of Africa.

Discussion on film production: March 2
Subject: The origins and development of cinema: technical, economic, and social.

Screening and discussion on film production: March 9
Subject: Films in relation to objective reality.
Films chosen from: *Unseen World*; *Vision – Structure of the Eye*; *Faster than Sound*; *Explorers of the Depths*; *Introduction to Sound*; *Explosions on the Sun* and *Sperm Cell Development in the Grasshopper*.

General screenings: March 9, 30
Hungry Miles. NFB of Canada (Canada), 1947.[5]
*Dances of the USSR.
The Battle of Russia. Why We Fight Series. Dir. Joris Ivens, Anato le Litvak and Frank Capra, U.S. Office of War Information (USA), 1943.

Discussion on film production: March 16
Subject: Films in relation to objective reality.

General screenings: March 16
As Old as the Hills. Dir. Allan Crick. Prod. John Halas. Technicolour Cartoon. Halas & Batchelor (UK), 1950.
*Layout and Handling in Factories. Crown Film Unit (UK), 1951.
Tanya. Dir. G.V. Alexandrov. Mosfilm (USSR), 1942
*The Task Before the Building Industry. Basic Films (UK), 1950.

Screening and discussion on film production: March 23
Subject: Film in relation to thought processes.
Films chosen from: *Brotherhood of Man* and excepts from *Ten Days That Shook the World*.

---

4   Realist Film Association membership was required for participation in discussion groups (February 1952, A series of discussions on FILM PRODUCTION, Realist Film Association pamphlet). However, later discussion groups became open to the general public.
5   March 9 only.

General screenings: March 23
*Battle for the Ukraine.
*Post Haste. Crown Film Unit (UK), 1951.
*The New Councillor. Crown Film Unit (UK), 1950.

Discussion on film production: March 30
Subject: Film in relation to thought processes.

General screenings: March 30
*Hungry Minds. NFB of Canada (Canada), 1947.

APRIL – MAY PROGRAM

Screening and discussion on film production: April 6
Subject: The relation of cinema to the other arts.
Films chosen from: *The Loon's Necklace; Julius Caesar; Van Gogh; Dances of the USSR; The Lady of the Camellias; The Marriage of Figaro* and *Hymn of the Nations*.

General screenings
April 6–27: *Daughters of China*. Dir. Zifeng Ling and Qiang Zhai. China Northeast Film Studio (People's Republic of China), 1949.

Discussion on film production: April 13
Subject: What is Art?

Screening and discussion on film production: April 20
Subject: Cinema and Theatre
Films chosen from: *Film Form, Eisenstein* – Chapters 'The Unexpected' and *Through Theatre to Cinema*.

Discussion on film production: April 27
Subject: Cinema in relation to literature, pictorial art and music.

General screenings
April 30 – May 25: *That Others May Live* (Border Street). Dir. Aleksander Ford. P.P. Film Polski (Poland), 1949.

Screening and discussion on film production: May 4
Subject: What is Realism?
Films chosen from: *Dots and Loops; The Children Must Learn; First Steps; Come Saturday* and *Metal Workers*.

Discussion on film production: May 11
Subject: What is Realism?

Screening and discussion on film production: May 18
Subject: What types of films are there?
Films chosen from: *Voyage Across the Impossible; At Land; Valley of the Tennessee; Your Children's Sleep* and *Family and Reality*.

Screening and discussion on film production: May 25
Subject: What types of films are there?
Films chosen from: *The Nose Has It; How to Sew Slide Fasteners; Life Begins; Latitude and Longitude; Children Growing Up with Other People; Mr Prokouk Makes a Film; Magic Canvas; Robinson Charley* and *Soviet Newsreel*.

MAY – JUNE PROGRAM

General screening: May 28 – June 22

White Haired Girl. Dir. Pu Wang and Hua Shui. China Northeast Film Studio (People's Republic of China), 1950.

Screening and discussion on film production: June 1
Subject: The script.
Films chosen from: *The City*; excepts from *Old Man Out* and *No Greater Love*.

Discussion on film production: June 8
Subject: The script

Screening and discussion on film production: June 15
Subject: Editing.
Films chosen from: *Study in Choreography for Camera; Film and Reality* and excerpts from *Great Expectations, The Overlanders* and *The Battleship Potemkin*.

Discussion on film production: June 22
Subject: Editing.

Screening and discussion on film production: June 29
Subject: Acting.
Films chosen from: Excerpts from *Mother* and *No Greater Love*.

JUNE – JULY PROGRAM

Discussion on film production: July 6
Subject: Acting.

Screening and discussion on film production: July 13
Subject: Camerawork – composition of the shot
Films chosen from: *Rhythm of a City; The Seashell and the Clergyman; Film and Reality* and excerpts from *Battleship Potemkin* and *Ten Days that Shook the World*.

General screening: June 25 – July 13
Oswiecim (The Last Stage). Dir. Wanda Jakubowski. Film Polski Production under auspices of the Film Board of the United Nations (Poland).

AUGUST - SEPTEMBER - OCTOBER PROGRAM

Scientific screenings
*Cotton. Dir. Lia Simonyi. Magyar Hiradó és Dokumentum Filmgyár (Hungary).
Vitamins ABC. Dir. Geoffrey Innes. Cambridge Film Productions (UK), 1937.

General screenings: 10-week season starting from August 20
Budapest Festival (Hungary).
Liberated Soil. Dir. Alexander Medvedkin. Sverdlovsk Studios (USSR), 1946.
**Life of the Beavers* (Czechoslovakia).
New Fighters Will Arise. Dir. Jiri Weiss. Czechoslovak State Film (Czechoslovakia), 1950.
The Strike. Dir. Karel Stekly. Czechoslovak State Film (Czechoslovakia), 1947.
Silent Barricades. Dir. Otakar Vávra. Filmové Studio Barrandov. Czechoslovak State Film (Czechoslovakia), 1949.

Theatre
October 29 – November 22: *Longitude*. Herb Tank, New Theatre.

NOVEMBER PROGRAM

General screenings
November 2: **Construction in Moscow* (USSR).
November 8 (special children's matinee): **Pioneer Palaces* (USSR) and *Lone White Sail* (USSR).
November 8, 9: *Lone White Sail*. Dir. Vladimir Legoshin. Mosfilm (USSR), 1938.
November 16: *Kameradschaft*. Dir. G.W. Pabst. Neo Film (Germany and France), 1931.
November 23, 26-30: **Song of a Happy Life (Singing Makes Life Beautiful)*. Musical Comedy (Hungary).

DECEMBER PROGRAM

End of year variety show: December 3–6
Organisational bodies: The Unity Dance Group; The Unity Singers; The New Theatre; The Realist Writers Group and the RFA.

REALIST FILM ASSOCIATION SCREENINGS 1953

In 1953 the 'RFA held 136 screenings of 24 feature films from eight countries to a combined audience of 1467… [and there were 294]… [s]creenings in suburban homes, halls and factories (*Realist Film News*: February – March 1953, Realist Film Association pamphlet, 3).

JANUARY – FEBRUARY PROGRAM

Tribute to Lenin program: January 21–25
The Battle of Russia. *Why We Fight* Series. Dir. Joris Ivens, Anato le Litvak and Frank Capra, U.S. Office of War Information (USA), 1943.
**Reconstruction of Moscow*. (USSR).

Tribute to Lenin program: January 28 – February 1
Battleship Potemkin. Dir. Sergei Eisenstein. First Studio Goskin. Silent (USSR), 1925.

Chinese Film Festival
February 4–8: *Daughters of China*. Dir. Zifeng Ling and Qiang Zhai. China Northeast Film Studio (People's Republic of China), 1949.
February 11–15: *The White Haired Girl*. Dir. Pu Wang and Hua Shui. China Northeast Film Studio (People's Republic of China), 1950.
February 18–22: *Liberated China*. Dir. Svetozarou Kuznetsov. Gorky Moscow Cine Studios (USSR in collaboration with the People's Republic of China), 1950.

MARCH PROGRAM

Theatre (Musical)
March 11 (four-week season due to popular demand extended to May): *Reedy River*. Richard Diamond, New Theatre.

Melbourne Film Festival: March 6–9
Held at Melbourne Exhibition Hall.

APRIL – MAY PROGRAM
The Baltic Deputy. Dir. Alexander Zherki and Josef Heifitz. Soviety Komsomol (Young Communist League) Film Brigade (USSR), c. mid-1930s.
**Soviet Kazakhstan*. Lydia Stepanova (USSR), 1951.

JUNE PROGRAM

Discussion group: June 6
Subject: Is cinema art?
How are they making the Coronation Films?

Special double feature program: nightly (except Mondays and Tuesdays) until June 28
The Tales of the Forest. Dir. Alexander Zguridi. Moscow Popular Science Film Studio (USSR), 1949.
A White Sail Gleams. Dir. V. Legoshin. Children's Cinema (Soyuzdetfilm) Studios (USSR), 1937.
RFA Advertising Commercial Release for the Savoy Theatre
**Concert of the Stars*. Leningrad Film Studios. Musical (USSR), 1952.
One Summer of Happiness. Dir. Arne Mattsson. Prod. Lennart Landheim. Nordisk Tonefilm (Sweden), 1951.

JULY PROGRAM
July 1–4: Variety Show.
July 5–12: **The Fight Will End Tomorrow*. Czechoslovak State Film (Czechoslovakia).
July 15–26: #*The Hwai River Must be Harnessed*. Dir. Mei Shih. Peing Film Studios (Peoples Republic of China), 1952.
July 15–26: *Deadline for Action*. Dir. Carl Marzani. Trade Union Movement. Union Films (USA), 1946.

AUGUST PROGRAM

Factory shows from August 1 – October 31 included:
Deadline for Action. Dir. Carl Marzani. Trade Union Movement. Union Films (USA), 1946.
*It Happened in May (Czechoslovakia).
The Tales of the Forest. Dir. Alexander Zguridi. Moscow Popular Science Film Studio (USSR), 1949.
The Battle of Russia. Why We Fight Series. Dir. Joris Ivens, Anato le Litvak and Frank Capra, U.S. Office of War Information (USA), 1943.
Documentaries and Newsreels.

SEPTEMBER PROGRAM

Two week tour of rural Victoria, screenings included:
*The Atom and You. Paramount News. Paramount Pictures (USA), 1952.
*Hungry Minds. NFB of Canada (Canada), 1947.
*Road to Peace.

General screenings
Lenin in October. Dir. Michael Romm. Mosfilm Production (USSR), 1937.
September 18–20: *Italian Straw Hat.* Dir. René Clair. Prod. Alexandre Kamenka. Films Albatros (France), 1927.
September 18–20: *Balzac.* Dir. Jean Vidal. A.F. Films (France), 1951.
September 25 – limited season: *Micky Magnate.* Dir. Márton Keleti. Hunnia Játékfilmstudió. Musical (Hungary), 1948.
September 25 – limited season: *Van Gogh.* Dir. Alain Resnais. Panthéon Productions (France), 1948.
September 25 – limited season: *World Record of Czech Athletes* (Czechoslovakia).

OCTOBER – NOVEMBER PROGRAM

 # Theatre production
Strangers in the Land written by Mona Brand.

General screenings
October 18: *Smiling Land.* Dir. Vaclav Gajer. Czech State Film Studio (Czechoslovakia), 1952.
October 25 and November 1: # *Village Rising.* Dir. Josef Mach. Czechoslovak State Film (Czechoslovakia), 1949.
November 8: *The Battle of Russia. Why We Fight* Series. Dir. Joris Ivens, Anato le Litvak and Frank Capra, U.S. Office of War Information (USA), 1943.
November 15, 22 and 29: **Oswiecim* (The Last Stage). Dir. Wanda Jakubowski. Film Polski Production under auspices of the Film Board of the United Nations (Poland).

Film appreciation evening: November 18[6]
Screening and informal discussion directed by Ken Coldicutt:

Film and Reality. Dir. Cavalcanti and Ernest Lindgren. National Film Library (Britain), 1942.

DECEMBER PROGRAM

General screenings
That Others May Live (Border Street). Dir. Aleksander Ford. P.P. Film Polski (Poland), 1949.
December 6: **It Happened in May* (Czechoslovakia).

Film appreciation evening: December 9
Screening and informal discussion directed by Ken Coldicutt:
Night Mail. Dir. and Prod. Harry Watt and Basil Wright. GPO Film Unit (UK), 1936.
*Come Saturday.

Special Christmas screening: December 18-20, 27 and January 3
*Tomorrow there will be Dancing Everywhere. Dir. Vladimír Vlcek. Czechoslovak State Film Studios (Czechoslovakia).

Soviet films (RFA Advertising Commercial Releases)
Grosevenor Theatre December 26: *Sadko.* Dir. Aleksander Ptushko. Sovexportfilm (USSR), 1952.
The Savoy: **Ukrainian Concert Hall* (to be shown with French film *Le Plaisir.* Dir. Max Ophulus. Prod. Edouard Harispuru. C.C.F.C. Stéra Films (France), 1951).

REALIST FILM ASSOCIATION SCREENINGS 1954

In 1954 '[a] total of 12,593 persons attended 99 New Theatre screenings… [and]… a total of 11,502 persons attended 192 suburban and factory shows' (Supplement to *Realist Film News*, March 1955, Realist Film Association pamphlet).

GENERAL PROGRAM
Man of Music.

JANUARY PROGRAM
Mrs Déry. Dir. Laszlo Kalmar. Hungarian State Films. Musical (Hungary), 1951.

Film appreciation evening: January 20
Informal discussion directed by Ken Coldicutt:
Cinema Scope and other widescreen processes.
Sadko. Dir. Aleksander Ptushko. Sovexportfilm (USSR), 1952.

FEBRUARY PROGRAM
February 5–7, 12–14: *The Proletarian Anna.* Dir. Karel Steklý. Czechoslovak State Film Production (Czechoslovakia), 1952.
February 19–21: *Mrs Déry.* Dir. Laszlo Kalmar. Hungarian State Films. Musical (Hungary), 1951.

---

6   These meetings were free and open to the general public, see: *Realist Film News* December 1952, Realist Film Association pamphlet.

February 26–28: *The Battle of Russia*. *Why We Fight* Series. Dir. Joris Ivens, Anato le Litvak and Frank Capra, U.S. Office of War Information (USA), 1943.

MARCH – APRIL PROGRAM

Film Forums: March 10, 24[7]
The origins and development of cinema.
The cinema in relation to objective reality.
Films chosen from: *Animated Cartoons* – the *Toy that Grew Up*; *Birth of a Motion Picture Camera*; *Bringing the World to the Classroom*; *Explorers of the Depths*; *Explosions on the Sun*; *Film and Reality*; *Introduction to Sound*; *March of the Movies*; *Unseen World* and *Vision – Structure of the Eye*.

Theatre
March 5 – April 24: *Trial By Falsehood*. Dir. Victor Arnold. New Theatre Players, New Theatre.

General screenings
March 7, 14: *That Others May Live (Border Street)*. Dir. Aleksander Ford. P.P. Film Polski (Poland), 1949.
March 17 (Free Preview): *Mitrea Cocor*. Dir. Marieta Sadova. Bucharest Cinema Studio Production (Romania), 1952.
March 21, 28: *Tomorrow there will be Dancing Everywhere*. Dir. Vladimír Vlcek. Czechoslovak State Film Studios (Czechoslovakia).
Tales of Hašek. Dir. Miroslav Hubaček. Czechoslovak State Films (Czechoslovakia), 1952.

APRIL – MAY PROGRAM

Film Forums: April 14, 28
Film in relation to thought processes.
Subject: Is film an art form?
Films chosen from: *Picture in Your Mind*; *Robinson Charley*; *Ten Days that Shook the World* and *The City*.

General screenings
April 4, 11: *Mitrea Cocor*. Dir. Marieta Sadova. Bucharest Cinema Studio Production (Romania), 1952.
April 7 (free preview): *Semmelweiss* (there are two possible records for this film):
1. *Semmelweiss*. Dir. André de Toth. Mester Film (Hungary), 1940.
2. *Semmelweiss*. Dir. Figyes Bán (Hungary), 1952.
April 18, 25: *Steel Town*. Dir. Martin Fric. Czechoslovak State Film Production (Czechoslovakia), 1954.

---

[7] At the February RFA Annual General Meeting it was decided that the Film Appreciation Meetings should be made into free regular fortnightly Film Forums (*Realist Film News* March 1954, Realist Film Association pamphlet, 3). As there are some discrepancies in RFA records regarding the running order for forum topics, for continuity topics in this document are taken from the following source: *Film Forum Realist Film News* March 1954 Supplement.

April 7–31: *Pensions for Veterans*. Dir. Keith Gow and Norma Disher. Waterside Workers' Federation Film Unit (Australia), 1953.
Weekly throughout May: *Semmelweis*.

Special May Day program
Showing throughout April and on May 1 and 2: *The Battle of Russia*. *Why We Fight* Series. Dir. Joris Ivens, Anato le Litvak and Frank Capra, U.S. Office of War Information (USA), 1943.
Mitrea Cocor. Dir. Marieta Sadova. Bucharest Cinema Studio Production (Romania), 1952.
Steel Town. Dir. Martin Fric. Czechoslovak State Film Production (Czechoslovakia), 1954.
Supporting feature throughout April: *Australian May Day 1953*. Realist Film Association (Australia).

Film Forum: May 12, 26
Subject: Film and Theatre
Film and Literature

Waterside Workers' Federation special program
The Atom and You. Paramount News. Paramount Pictures (USA), 1952.
Native Land. Dir. Leo Hurwitz and Paul Strand. Frontier Films (USA), 1942.
Pensions for Veterans. Dir. Keith Gow and Norma Disher. Waterside Workers' Federation Film Unit (Australia), 1953.

Classes
Free weekly projection classes.

Melbourne Film Festival: May 31 – June 19

JUNE PROGRAM

General screenings
June 2 (preview): Soviet Colour Animation – unknown title.
June 4–6: *The Battle of Russia*. *Why We Fight* Series. Dir. Joris Ivens, Anato le Litvak and Frank Capra, U.S. Office of War Information (USA), 1943.
June 11–13, 18–20: *Louisiana Story*. Dir. Robert Flaherty. Robert Flaherty Productions, Inc., 1947-8.
June 11–13, 18–20: *Fish and the Fisherman*. Artkino. Colour Animation (USSR), 1950.
June 25–27: *That Others May Live (Border Street)*. Dir. Aleksander Ford. P.P. Film Polski (Poland), 1949.

Film Forum: June 9, 23
Subject: Film and graphic arts
Film and music

JULY PROGRAM

General screenings
July 4, 11: *The Cavalier of the Gold Star*. Dir. Julius Raizman. Mosfilm Production (USSR), 1951.

July 18: *Oswiecim (The Last Stage)*. Dir. Wanda Jakubowski. Film Polski Production under auspices of the Film Board of the United Nations (Poland).
July 25: *The Battle of Russia*. Why We Fight Series. Dir. Joris Ivens, Anato le Litvak and Frank Capra, U.S. Office of War Information (USA), 1943.

Film Forum: July 14, 28
Subject: What is Realism?
What kinds of film are there?
International Film Festival Czechoslovakia
RFA representative: Cecil Holmes

AUGUST PROGRAM

General screenings
August 1, 8: *Steel Town*. Dir. Martin Fric. Czechoslovak State Film Production (Czechoslovakia), 1954.
August 15, 22: *Kameradschaft*. Dir. G.W. Pabst. Neo Film (Germany and France), 1931.
August 27–29: *Native Land*. Dir. Leo Hurwitz and Paul Strand. Frontier Films (USA), 1942.

Film Forum: August 11, 25
Subject: The Script.
Editing.

SEPTEMBER PROGRAM

General screenings
September 4–5, 18–19: *Native Land*. Dir. Leo Hurwitz and Paul Strand. Frontier Films (USA), 1942.
September 10–12: *The Blue Angel*. Dir. Joseph von Sternberg. Prod. Eric Pommer at UFA (Germany), 1929.
September 24–26: *The Young Guard*. Dir. Sergei Gerasimov. Gorky Studio (USSR), 1948.

Film Forum: September 8, 22
Camerawork
Sound: screening extracts from *Children Must Learn*; *Pictures in Your Mind* and *Loops*.

OCTOBER PROGRAM

General screenings
October 1–3: *Louisiana Story*. Dir. Robert Flaherty. Robert Flaherty Productions, Inc. (USA), 1947-8.
October 8–10 (for members): *À Nous La Liberte (Freedom for Us)*. Dir. René Clair. Tobis (France), 1931.
October 15–17: *Land of Promise*. Dir. Paul Rotha. Films of Fact Production (UK), 1945.
October 22–24, 31: *The Battle of Russia*. Why We Fight Series. Dir. Joris Ivens, Anato le Litvak and Frank Capra. U.S. Office of War Information (USA), 1943.

Film Forum: October 13, 27
Subject: Colour: screening extracts from: *Pictures in Your Mind*; *Magic Cameras* and *Make Fruitful the Land*.
Stereoscopy.

NOVEMBER PROGRAM

Friendship with Asia month: November 7, 14
Indonesia Calling. Dir. Joris Ivens. Prod. for the Waterside Workers' Federation of Australia. Australasia Productions (Australia), 1946.
Liberated China. Dir. Svetozarou Kuznetsov. Gorky Moscow Cine Studios (USSR in collaboration with the People's Republic of China), 1950.

Friendship with Asia month: November 10, 24

Films from India – documentaries and newsreels.
No Greater Love. Dir. Frederick Ermler. Alma Ata Studios (USSR), 1943.
15 special screenings in suburban homes and halls: *The White Haired Girl*. Dir. Pu Wang and Hua Shui. China Northeast Film Studio (People's Republic of China), 1950.

Film Forum: November 10, 24
Subject: Television
A Summing-up.

DECEMBER PROGRAM

General screening
Battleship Potemkin. Dir. Sergei Eisenstein. First Studio Goskin. Silent (USSR), 1925.
Men of the Mulga. Dir. and Prod. Hamilton Aikin. Presbyterian Board of Missions (Australia), 1953.
Native Land. Dir. Leo Hurwitz and Paul Strand. Frontier Films (USA), 1942.
That Others May Live (Border Street). Dir. Aleksander Ford. P.P. Film Polski (Poland), 1949.

REALIST FILM ASSOCIATION SCREENINGS 1955

In 1955 '28 feature films… [were shown]… to a total of 12,840 persons at New Theatre. The number of screenings was 97… In suburban areas 5795 persons attended 34 screenings… The most successful… were outside screenings at the seaside resort of Rosebud where the Cheltenham Film Society showed some of our films to as many as 1100 persons per show. Other groups used our films, equipment, projectionists and other facilities… [these included]… peace groups, church organisations, school and kindergarten parents' societies, and a number of national groups. The Builders' Laborers' [sic] on-the-job screenings… have been especially successful… [holding]… 78 shows' (*Realist Film News*, March – April 1956, Realist Film Association pamphlet).

General screenings
Chuk and Gek. Dir. Ivan Lukinsky. Gorky Film Studios (USSR), 1953.

His Loyal Highness. Dir. F. W. Thring. Efftee Film Productions (Australia), 1932.
Song of Man. Dir. Borislav Sharaliev. Boyana Film (Bulgaria), 1954.
*Tales from Hasek (Czechoslovakia).
The Battle of Russia. Why We Fight Series. Dir. Joris Ivens, Anato le Litvak and Frank Capra, U.S. Office of War Information (USA), 1943.
*The Café in the Main Street. Dir. Miroslav Hubucek. Czechoslovak State Film (Czechoslovakia).
The Quiet One. Dir. Sidney Meyers. Film Documents, Inc. (USA), 1949.
Youth of the World. Dir. Herbert Brieger and Carl Junghans. Propaganda-Ausschuss für die Olypische Spiele (USSR-German), 1936.

JANURAY PROGRAM
Battleship Potemkin. Dir. Sergei Eisenstein. First Studio Goskin. Silent (USSR), 1925.
*Mr Angel takes a Holiday. Dir. Borivoj Zeman (Czechoslovakia).
*Songs and Dances of the People.

Classes
Beginner's weekly projection class begins.
Advanced weekly projection class begins.

FEBRUARY PROGRAM
The Secret of Blood. Martin Frič. Czechoslovak State Film (Czechoslovakia), 1953.

Film Forum: February 16[8]
Screening and discussion
Battleship Potemkin. Dir. Sergei Eisenstein. First Studio Goskin. Silent (USSR), 1925.

MARCH PROGRAM

Public previews of State Film Centre Films: Nicholas Hall March 15[9]
Invisible Link. Dir. Victor Vicas. Victor Vicas Films (France), 1950.
*First Steps. United Nations Film Board (International Agencies), 1948.
*Playing with Fire.
The Steps of Age. Dir. Ben Maddow. Prod. Helen Levitt. Film Documents Productions (USA), 1951.
*Ages and Stages: Terrible Twos and Trusting Threes. Crawley Films. NFB (Canada), 1950.
V for Volunteers. Dir. Leslie McFarlane. NFB (Canada), 1951.
**Your Child is a Genius*. David Robbins Productions (USA).

General Screenings
March 4–6, 13: *Mrs Déry*. Dir. Laszlo Kalmar. Hungarian State Films. Musical (Hungary), 1951.
March 20: *Conquest of Everest*. Dir. Thomas Stobart. Countryman Films. Group 3 (UK), 1953.
March 27: *New Fighters Will Arise*. Dir. Jiri Weiss. Czechoslovak State Film (Czechoslovakia), 1950.

APRIL PROGRAM
April 3, 10: *Bim*. Dir. Albert Lamorisse. Films Marceau (France), 1951.
April 3, 10: *The Heart is Highland*. Dir. John Taylor. Prod. Edgar Anstey. British Transport Films (UK), 1952.

MAY PROGRAM
Children of Hiroshima (Atom Bomb Children). Dir. Káneto Shindo. Prod. Kíndai Éiga. Modern Cinema Association and Theatre Group People's Art (Japan), 1952.
Forum: May 11

JUNE PROGRAM
June 10–12: *Ivan the Terrible*. Dir. Sergei M. Eisenstein. Mosfilm (USSR), 1945.
June 17–19: **Time in the Sun*. Eisenstein. Prod. Marie Seton (USA), 1938.
June 17–19: *Zéro de Conduite*. Dir. J. Vigo. Prod. Jacques-Louis Nounez. Argui-Film (France), 1933.
June 22, 26: *Le Million*. René Claire. Films Sonores Tobis (France), 1931.

Film Forum: June 22
Le Million.

JULY – AUGUST PROGRAM
August 7: **Marusya's First Year in School* (USSR)
August 14: *Conquest of Everest*. Dir. Thomas Stobart. Countryman Films. Group 3 (UK), 1953.
August 21, 28: *A Ticket in Tatts*. Dir. Frank Thring. Efftee Film Productions (Australia), 1934.

SEPTEMBER PROGRAM
September 2–4, 9–11: *Crin Blanc, Cheval Sauvage (The White Horse White Mane)*. Albert Lamorisse. Les films Montsouris (France), 1953.
September 2–4, 9–11: *Hungry Miles*. Prod. Jereome Levy and Keith Gow. Waterside Workers' Federation of Australia (Australia), 1955.
September 2–4, 9–11: **Song of Youth* (German and USSR collaboration).
September 16–18: *Centre Forward*. Dir. S. Derevyansky and I. Zemgano. Kiev Studios (USSR), 1946.
September 21: *The Sentimental Bloke*. Dir. Raymond Longford. Southern Cross Features Film Company (Australia), 1918.
September 23–25: *Children of Hiroshima (Atom Bomb Children)*. Dir. Káneto Shíndo. Prod. Kíndai Éiga. Modern Cinema Association and Theatre Group People's Art (Japan), 1952.
First National Conference of Australian Realist Film Groups.

---

8   To be held every second Wednesday throughout the year.
9   It is uncertain as to whether these were RFA screenings, or the RFA was simply advertising the films in their leaflet.

OCTOBER – NOVEMBER PROGRAM

Ocean Grove weekend: November 4
Film weekend held by Federation of Victorian Film Societies.

NOVEMBER SCREENINGS (SUNDAYS ONLY)
November Victory. Dir. Jock Levy, Keith. Gow and Norma Disher. Waterside Workers' Federation of Australia Film Unit (Australia), 1955.
November 6: *Lenin in October*. Mikhail Romm. Mosfilm (USSR), 1937.
November 13, 27: *Intolerance*. Dir. D. W. Griffith. Triangle Film Corporation. Silent (USA), 1916.
November 20: *Children of Hiroshima (Atom Bomb Children)*. Dir. Káneto Shíndo. Prod. Kíndai Éiga. Modern Cinema Association and Theatre Group People's Art (Japan), 1952.

Film Forum

November 16 topic: The Australian Scene
The Valley is Ours. Dir. John Heyer. NFB (Australia), 1948.

November 30 topic: Cavalcade of Australia
*Story of a Country
Snowy Waters. Dir. Bern Gandy. Prod. John Martin-Jones. Film Division, Department of the Interior (Australia), 1952.
Cavalcade of Australia. Dir. Shan Benson and Hugh McInnes. Australian Commonwealth Film Unit (Australia), 1951.

REALIST FILM ASSOCIATION SCREENINGS 1956

In 1956 'New Theatre screenings consisted of 77 seasons of evening shows (audience: 8270), six matinees (audience: 224), four special shows (audience: 232) and 27 Sunday night shows (audience: 4392). The total number of people who attended the New Theatre shows was 13,118... In addition to New Theatre shows, we conducted, or were associated with, 164 shows attended by 14,808 persons' (*Realist Film News*: February 1957, Realist Film Association pamphlet).

GENERAL PROGRAM
Bones of Building. Dir. Cecil Holmes. Australian Tradition Films (Australia).
Chuk and Gek. Dir. Ivan Lukinsky. Gorky Film Studios (USSR), 1953.
Indonesia Calling. Dir. Joris Ivens. Prod. for the Waterside Workers' Federation of Australia. Australasia Productions (Australia), 1946.
Inseparable Friends. Dir. Vasili Zhuravlyov. Kiev Film Studios (USSR), 1952.
Japanese Fisherman.
Relatives. Dir. Félix Máriássy. Magyar Filmgyártó Vallalat (Hungary), 1954.

JANUARY PROGRAM
The Cannery Boat. Contemporary Productions (Japan).

Wharf strike special screenings: January 25
Hungry Miles. Prod. Jereome Levy and Keith Gow. Waterside Workers' Federation of Australia (Australia), 1955.
The Song of the Rivers. Dir. and Prod. Joris Ivens. World Federation of Trade Unions. DEFA Studios (East Germany), 1954.

Workers' Film Group
Children of Hiroshima (Atom Bomb Children). Dir. Káneto Shíndo. Prod. Kíndai Éiga. Modern Cinema Association and Theatre Group People's Art (Japan), 1952.

FEBRUARY PROGRAM

General screenings
The Council of the Gods. Dir. Kurt Maetzig. DEFA Studios (East Germany), 1950.

Screening for crew of Japanese ship 'S.S. Yukikawa Maru': February 11
Pensions for Veterans. Dir. Keith Gow and Norma Disher. Waterside Workers' Federation Film Unit (Australia), 1953.
The Art of Judo. (Japan).
The Cannery Boat. Contemporary Productions (Japan):

MARCH PROGRAM

General screenings
The Song of the Rivers. Dir. and Prod. Joris Ivens. World Federation of Trade Unions. DEFA Studios (East Germany), 1954.
The Salt of the Earth. Dir. Herbert J. Biberman. Independent Productions of Hollywood and the International Union of Mine, Mill and Smelter Workers of America (USA), 1953.

Discussion nights: March 7, 14:
Screening and discussion of RFA member Dr. A. Dobbin's trip through China and Soviet Union.

APRIL PROGRAM

General screening
San Demetrio London. Dir. Charles Frend. Prod. Michael Balcon. Ealing Studios (UK), 1943.
April 8: *The Battle of Russia*. Why We Fight Series. Dir. Joris Ivens, Anato le Litvak and Frank Capra, U.S. Office of War Information (USA), 1943.

Second National Conference of Realist Film Groups: held in Sydney over the Easter weekend.

MAY – JUNE PROGRAM

General screenings
Childhood of Maxim Gorki. Dir. Mark Donskoi. Soyuzdetfilm. Trilogy (USSR), 1937-9.

Young Chopin. Dir. Aleksander Ford. Film Polski (Poland), 1952.
Hiroshima Panels (Portrait of the Atom Bomb). Dir. Tadashi Imai (Japan), 1954.

Melbourne Film Festival: May 21 – June 10

JULY PROGRAM

July 15, 22 (including matinee): *The Proud Princess*. Dir. Borivoj Zeman. Czechoslovak State Film (Czechoslovakia), 1952.
July 15, 22 (including matinee): Charlie Chaplin film: unknown title.
July 29: **Butterfly Lovers*. Ministry of Culture (People's Republic of China), c.1950s.

AUGUST – SEPTEMBER PROGRAM

General screenings
Liberated China. Dir. Svetozarou Kuznetsov. Gorky Moscow Cine Studios (USSR in collaboration with the People's Republic of China), 1950.
November Victory. Dir. Jock Levy, Keith. Gow and Norma Disher. Waterside Workers' Federation of Australia Film Unit (Australia), 1955.
The Proud Princess. Dir. Borivoj Zeman. Czechoslovak State Film (Czechoslovakia), 1952.
Treasure. Dir. Leonard Buczkowski. Prod. Ludwik Hager. Film Polski (Poland), 1949.
Two Acres of Land. Dir. Bimal Roy. Bimal Roy Productions (India), 1953.
August 1 (free preview): *Relatives*. Dir. Félix Máriássy. Magyar Filmgyártó Vallalat (Hungary), 1954.
August 19, 26: *Hiroshima Panels (Portrait of the Atom Bomb)*. Dir. Tadashi Imai (Japan), 1954.
September 7–9: *Le Jour Se Léve (Break of Day)*. Dir. Marcel Carné. Productions Sigma (France), 1939.
September 7–9: *Lenin in October*. Dir. Michael Romm. Mosfilm Production (USSR), 1937.
September 14–16: *M. Hulot's Holiday*. Dir. Jacques Tati. Cady Films (France), 1953.
September 14–16: *Mrs Déry*. Dir. Laszlo Kalmar. Hungarian State Films. Musical (Hungary), 1951.
September 21–23: *Bread Love and Dreams*. Dir. Luigi Comencini. Titanus (Italy), 1953.
September 28–30: **River Lights* (USSR).

Previews: September 5
Short films previewed at quarterly general meeting topics: May Day and WWF strike (titles unknown).

First members night: September 12[10]
Screenings:
Let's Talk About Films. Dir. Julian Biggs. NFB (Canada), 1953.

World Without End. Dir. Paul Rotha. Prod. Basil Wright. International Realist (Britain), 1953.
Operation Hurricane. Dir. Ronald Stark. Prod. Stuart Legg. Atomic Weapons Research Establishment (Britain), 1952.
Neighbours. Dir. and Prod. Norman McLaren. NFB. Animation (Canada), 1952.

OCTOBER PROGRAM

General screenings: October 5–7
St. Martin's Lane. Dir. Tim Whelan. Prod. Erich Pommer. Mayflowers Pictures Corporation (UK), 1938.
Tales of Hašek. Dir. Miroslav Hubaček. Czechoslovak State Films (Czechoslovakia), 1952.
That Others May Live (Border Street). Dir. Aleksander Ford. P.P. Film Polski (Poland), 1949.
The Tales of the Forest. Dir. Alexander Zguridi. Moscow Popular Science Film Studio (USSR), 1949.

Discussion night
Australian director and producer Cecil Holmes gave a report on his trip to the Karlovy Vary, Edinburgh and Cannes Film Festivals.

NOVEMBER PROGRAM

November 18: *Young Chopin*. Dir. Aleksander Ford. Film Polski (Poland), 1952.
November 18: *Three in One*. Dir. Cecil Holmes. Australian Tradition Films (Australia).
November 18: *Words for Freedom*.
November 25: *Soviet Whalers*. Dir. L. Setkina. Central Documentary Studios (USSR), 1951.

Special screening for members and their guests: November 28
A Cottage on Dartmoor. Dir. Anthony Asquith. Prod. Bruce H. Woolfe. British Instructional Films (UK), 1929.
NB: By the end of 1956 RFA extra activities included:
Film production
Free classes on production and projection
Regular discussion meetings on the film
A well-stocked library of books on the film
Sale of books and magazines on the film, and the publication of brochures on various aspects of the film
Socials, previews, etc (*Realist Film News*, July 1956, Realist Film Association pamphlet).

REALIST FILM ASSOCIATION SCREENINGS 1957

MEMBERS PROGRAM[11]
Screenings for 1957 included:
Broken Blossoms. Dir. John Brahm. Prod. Julius Hagen. Twickenham Film Studios Productions (UK), 1936.

---

10   The members night was held every Wednesday evening at the New Theatre (*Realist Film News* August 1956, Realist Film Association Pamphlet).

11   Monthly screenings of films classics for members only.

The Cabinet of Dr Caligari. Dir. Robert Wiene. Silent. (Germany), 1951.
General Line (The Old and the New), Sergei M. Eisenstein. Soukino (USSR), 1929.
Kameradschaft. Dir. G.W. Pabst. Neo Film (Germany and France), 1931.
Man of Aran. Dir. Robert Flaherty and Prod. Michael Balcon. Gainsborough Pictures (UK), 1934.
Metropolis. Dir. Fritz Land. Prod. Erich Pommer. UFA (Germany), 1927.
Mother (there are two possible records for this film):
1. *Mother*. Vsevolod Pudovkin. Silent (USSR),1926.
2. *Mother*. Dir. James Leo Meehan. R-C Pictures (USA), 1927.
**Nanook of the North*. Dir. and Prod. Robert Flaherty (Canada), 1921.
Italian Straw Hat. Dir. René Clair. Prod. Alexandre Kamenka. Films Albatros (France), 1927.
The Last Laugh. F.W. Murnau. Silent (Germany), 1924.

General screenings
Daring Circus Youth. Dir. Sergei Gurov and Yuri Ozerov. Mosfilm (USSR), 1953.
Gorky Trilogy. Dir. Mark Donskoy. Soyuzdetfilm (USSR), 1938, 1939, 1940.
**Inside the German Wars*.
The Magic Sword. Dir. Vojislav Nanovic. Zvezda Film (Former Yugoslavia), 1950.
*Windy Mountain.

MARCH PROGRAM
March 3, 10 and 17: *The Sentimental Bloke*. Dir. Raymond Longford. Southern Cross Features Film Company (Australia), 1918.

JULY – OCTOBER PROGRAM
July 14: *Pickwick Papers*. Dir. and Prod. Noel Langley. Renown Pictures Corporation (UK), 1952.
July 21: *Ivan the Terrible*. Dir. Sergei M. Eisenstein. Mosfilm (USSR), 1945.
July 26–28: *Storm Over Asia (Heir to Genghtz Khan 1928)*. Dir. Pudovkin. Re-issued with sound (USSR), 1949.
August 2–4: *Romeo and Juliet (USSR).
August 7: **Nanook of the North*. Dir. and Prod. Robert Flaherty (Canada) 1921.
August 9–11: *Diary of a Country Priest*. Dir. Robert Bresson. Prod. Léon Carré. U.G.C. (France), 1951.
August 16–18: *Frenzy*. Dir. Alf Sjöberg. Sjöberg-Bergman Group (Sweden), 1944.
September 4: **The Cabinet of Dr Caligari*. Dir. Robert Wiene. Silent. (Germany), 1951.
Throughout October: *Pather Panchali*. Dir. Satyajit Ray. Government of West Bengal. Part I: Apu Trilogy (India), 1955.
October 2: *General Line (The Old and the New)*, Sergei M. Eisenstein. Soukino (USSR), 1929.
Projection Classes: October 14

NOVEMBER PROGRAM
November 6: *Kameradschaft*. Dir. G.W. Pabst. Neo Film (Germany and France), 1931.
November 1–3, 20, 27: *Alexander Nevsky*. Dir. Sergei M. Eisenstein. Mosfilm (USSR), 1955.
November 8–10, 13: *Jan Hus*. Dir. Otakar Vávra. Czechoslovak State Films. Part I of III (Czechosolvakia), 1955.
November 15–17, 24: *Othello*. Dir. Sergi Yutkevitch, Mosfilm (USSR), 1955.

REALIST FILM ASSOCIATION SCREENINGS 1958

MEMBERS PROGRAM[12]

Screenings for 1958 included (not exclusive):
*A Divided World.
Bim. Dir. Albert Lamorisse. Films Marceau (France), 1951.
Bow Bells. Dir. Anthony Simmons and Leon Clore. Harlequin Productions (UK), 1954.

Cartoons and animated films: titles unknown.
Crin Blanc, Cheval Sauvage (The White Horse White Mane). Albert Lamorisse. Les films Montsouris (France), 1953.
**Critic and the Film: Odd Man Out*. Basil Wright.
*David.
Farrebique. George Rouquier. Ecran Francais (France), 1946.

Films from Melbourne Film Festival: titles unknown.
Fires Were Started. Humphrey Jennings. Crown Film Unit (UK), 1943.
Introduction to Jazz. Dir. Denis Sanders. UCLA School of Theatre, Film and Television (USA), 1952.
La Passion de Jeanne D'Arch. Dir. Carl-Teodore Dreyer. Société Generale de Films (France), 1927.
On Our Selection (there are two possible records for this film):
1. *On Our Selection. Dir. Raymond Longford (Australia), 1920.
2. *On Our Selection*. Dir. Ken G. Hall. Cinesound Productions Limited (Australia), 1932.
Le Sang Des Bétes. Dir. Georges Franju. Forces et Voixde (France), 1948.
Muscle Beach. Dir. Irving Lerner and Joseph Strick. Strick Film Company (USA), 1948.
Safety Last. Dir. Fred Newmeyer and Sam Taylor. Pathé Exchange (USA), 1923.
*Time in the Sun. Eisenstein. Prod. Marie Seton (USA), 1938.
**The Ascent of Eiffel*.
**The Gentlemen in Room 6*.
The Lodger. Dir. Alfred Hitchcock. Gainsborough Pictures (UK), 1926.

---

12 Monthly screenings of films classics for members only.

The Quiet One. Dir. Sidney Meyers. Film Documents, Inc. (USA), 1949.
The Undefeated. Dir. Paul Dickson. Prod. James Carr. World Wide Pictures (UK), 1950.
*Three American Ballads (USA), 1952.
Un Jardin Public. Dir. Paul Paviot. Prod. Madeleine Rodriguez Casanova. Pavox Film (France), 1956.

GENERAL PROGRAM

*Hewers of Coal. Miners Federation. WWF Film Unit (Australia), 1953.
*One Summer of Happiness (Sweden).
The Anna Cross. Dir. Isidor Annensky. Gorki Studio Film (USSR), 1954.
The Impostor. Dir. Tatsuo Osone. Shochiku Co. Ltd. Productions (Japan), 1952.

JANUARY – MARCH PROGRAM

General screenings
January 5: *Jan Hus*. Dir. Otakar Vávra. Czechoslovak State Films. Part I of III (Czechosolvakia).
March 2: *Eleven from our Block*. Dir. Alexei Maslyukov. Kiev Film Studios (USSR), 1953.
March 5: *The Quiet One*. Dir. Sidney Meyers. Film Documents, Inc. (USA), 1949.
March 9: **Inside the German Wars*.
March 12, 16: *Young Chopin*. Dir. Aleksander Ford. Film Polski (Poland), 1952.
March 19, 23: *Battleship Potemkin*. Dir. Sergei Eisenstein. First Studio Goskin. Silent (USSR), 1925.
March 26, 30: **Oswiecim (The Last Stage)*. Dir. Wanda Jakubowski. Film Polski Production under auspices of the Film Board of the United Nations (Poland).

Projection classes: March 3

BIBLIOGRAPHY

BFI Film and TV Database, available from: http://ftvdb.bfi.org.uk

National Film Board Canada Database, available from: http://www.nfb.ca

National Film and Sound Archive (Australia), available from: http://www.nfsa.gov.au

Realist Film Association leaflets, correspondence and promotional materials between the years 1946 – 1958.

The Internet Movie Database, available from: http://www.imdb.com